# HAUNTED
## SPRINGFIELD,
## ILLINOIS

# HAUNTED
# SPRINGFIELD,
# ILLINOIS

## GARRET MOFFETT

### REVISED, EXPANDED AND UPDATED

Published by Haunted America
A Division of The History Press
Charleston, SC
www.historypress.com

ISBN 9781467156837

Library of Congress Control Number: 2024936747

*This book is dedicated to the Trinity.*
*The Father, the Son and the Holy Ghost.*
*The Spirit has got me this far.*

# CONTENTS

# ACKNOWLEDGEMENTS

My thanks to the Sangamon Valley Collection, the Abraham Lincoln Presidential Library, the Illinois Department of Natural Resources, the National Park Service, the *State Journal-Register*, Conn's Hospitality, the Springfield Ghost Society, the Capitol Area Paranormal Society and all of the people who contributed but wish to remain anonymous.

# LINCOLN'S NEW SALEM

A pioneer named Jack Kelso is thought to be one of the first to arrive on the forested bluff just above the Sangamon River, in 1825. He was a hunter and a trapper. Soon others arrived, and before long, a hamlet of log homes had become the village of New Salem.

Waterways were the main method of getting merchandise and agriculture products to markets in 1830s America. Railroads would not be established for another twenty-five years. The riverboats on the Mississippi and Illinois Rivers were widely used to get products to market. Villagers in New Salem were able to convince legislators to dam up the Sangamon River to raise water levels. Then the smaller riverboats could make it up the Sangamon River from the Illinois River. The villagers could then transport and sell their agriculture and crafted items at market. Increasing river commerce was desirable to the legislators. In 1829, the Sangamon River had a dam built with a saw- and gristmill over the top of it, and the Port of New Salem was created. With the new river commerce potential, more people began to arrive and began building log homes in New Salem. Before long, it had become a bustling little growing village of about three hundred people at its peak.

Abraham Lincoln would be the most famous resident who came to New Salem when he arrived in 1831 at just twenty-one years old. Lincoln said that he arrived here as "an aimless piece of driftwood." But Lincoln would make his mark in life while at New Salem. He volunteered in the Black Hawk War, became a land surveyor and the postmaster general and had ownership in a general store. Lincoln also studied law under the tutelage of John Todd Stuart, a cousin to his future wife. And in New Salem, Lincoln made his first run at political office.

In any village, a blacksmith is a must, but so is a general store for supplies, a doctor, a tavern for weary travelers needing a meal and a bunk for the night. But there was also a post office, a carding mill, a grocery store, a school that doubled as a church, a stagecoach stop and even a cooper shop for making barrels and buckets. Today, the cooper shop of Henry Onstot is the only original building in the park. This is the workshop where Lincoln studied his law books by the firelight at night.

Although New Salem had all the makings of a successful growing community, unfortunately by 1837 only one riverboat had made it on the Sangamon River to New Salem, and Lincoln had left town for Springfield to pursue his law career there. Soon after, river levels dropped, and the river never recovered without any known cause. With low water levels and boats unable to navigate the river, New Salem received its death knell. The village would gradually die off, unable to make a living off the river commerce. Residents slowly left, and abandoned homes succumbed to vegetation and rot over time. New Salem became a ghost town—after nearly two hundred years, in more ways than one.

This rebuilt 1830s pioneer village is about seventeen miles north of Springfield. New Salem first became a state park in 1921. The village was rebuilt by the Civilian Conservation Corps in 1930, with log homes reconstructed on the original foundations. Today, the rebuilt village is a magical place where the history comes alive with reenactors in period 1830s dress demonstrating pioneer village life. The history here is long and complex, and discoveries are still being made today. If life from the past could be in the present, here would be the place.

Inexplicable encounters with the historical past have been experienced by staff and tourists alike. Some of the reported experiences by tourists are similar to stories told by staff whose paths have never crossed. Perhaps there are old ghosts that remain within the rebuilt homes on original foundations and along the old trails, their lives forever imprinted onto the environment by a tragedy or failed hopes of prosperity.

Is New Salem haunted by Abraham Lincoln? There's the occasional visitor who believes that they've seen a spectral bearded Lincoln in stovepipe hat sauntering his way through the village. But these stories are quite suspect, as Lincoln did not have a full beard or wear a stovepipe hat until years later in his Springfield days. However, more credible tales of ghostly old villagers

*Top*: The Kelso-Miller dogtrot-style log home and the Miller blacksmith shop next door. *Garret Moffett.*

*Bottom*: The Herndon log home, where Herndon accidentally shot and killed his wife. *Garret Moffett.*

going about their business in the homes and throughout the village have been told for years by park staff, volunteers and visitors.

A well-known ghost story involves the home of Jack Kelso. He was thought to one of the first settlers to arrive. He had an unusual log home built in the "dogtrot" style, which is two opposing homes connected by a

The Rutledge Tavern, where weary travelers could get a meal and a bunk for the night. *Garret Moffett.*

common breezeway separating the two homes but with a single roof. Jack Kelso lived on one side, and Joshua Miller, who was married to Jack's sister, lived on the other side. Miller's blacksmith shop was right next door. A visiting couple casually walking through the park one evening after closing time noticed what they thought was a costumed interpreter leaning against the front of the Kelso home. Looking as if he was from early pioneer days, he had a wide soft brim hat covering his eyes. His arms were folded, and his head was tilted down; he just seemed really unusual in his appearance to them. The way he was leaning back against the home gave the impression that he didn't have a care in the world. But there was something inviting about this character, so the couple decided to walk over to him and say hello. As they approached, the man began to lift his head as if he were acknowledging their approach, but then, much to their amazement, he suddenly faded out of their sight without explanation. The astonished couple thought it odd that there would be costumed interpreters in the park after hours, which is still open to walk through. Others have reported seeing a similar ghostly figure in the vicinity of the Kelso home, with most stories coming from people walking or out for a run through the park in the evenings. Staff is skeptical of stories and protective, of course, but at least one volunteer working at the Kelso home during the day claimed that as she walked up to the home to work, she saw the back side of a man stepping into the Kelso home, so she stepped right up to the breezeway to tell the man that no one is supposed to be inside the home without her. But as she looked into the home, she saw no one present; she also noticed that the rocking chair in the breezeway was rocking a little, catching her off guard and making her a little nervous. But one thing staff will agree on is that if any old villagers are haunting New Salem, it sure would be Jack Kelso, the first pioneer to arrive and the last to finally leave the doomed village. But it would seem that he still might be around from time to time.

Perhaps the most well-known ghostly story from New Salem is the ghost of Elizabeth Herndon, who died a tragic death on the early morning of January 18, 1833, under questionable circumstances, according to some of the villagers. Her husband, Rowan, was getting ready to go out hunting that morning. Lincoln was doing some work on the nearby Rutledge Tavern, as he frequently did. But he needed a particular tool, so Lincoln sent young Nancy Rutledge over to the Herndon home to borrow the tool. When Nancy entered the home, she saw Mr. Herndon loading his rifle. Nancy's back was to Mr. Herndon while she was explaining to Elizabeth what she needed to get for Lincoln. Suddenly, without warning, the rifle fired and struck Elizabeth Herndon in the neck. In full panic, Nancy ran out of the home back over to the tavern to get help. Lincoln ran back over with Nancy and others to the Herndon home, where some say Lincoln cradled Mrs. Herndon in his lap on the floor until she died moments later. The bullet hit an artery, so blood was everywhere. Mr. Herndon claimed that the rifle slipped off his boot while he was loading it when it fired and hit his wife by accident. Herndon faced suspicions by some of the villagers who wondered why he wasn't trying to help his wife when Lincoln burst into the home and tried to save her. Whatever the case, it's quite possible that he was in shock over what he had done unexpectedly by accident and was unable to respond. Herndon, nevertheless, was devastated by the loss of his wife and left New Salem for good.

One afternoon, a tourist family was exploring through the village and were walking past the old Herndon home when the young girl told her parents that she liked the old-looking dress the lady was wearing in front of the door of the log home. Her parents didn't see anyone standing there, and the mom asked her daughter who she was referring to. The girl responded, "That lady right there, standing on the step in front of the door." Still seeing no one, the father walked over to the home several feet away, thinking that whomever she saw stepped inside the home, but when he tried the door, it was closed and locked. The family brushed it off as the imagination of their young daughter. Later, the family were explaining to staff about how they enjoyed the park and their daughter's active imagination walking past the Herndon home. They were told about the Herndon tragedy and the ghostly sightings that have occasionally occurred there. Was that Mrs. Herndon standing in front of the door? Children are often accused of having active imaginations. However, due to their open minds and innocence, children are also thought to be susceptible to ghostly encounters. Perhaps the young girl had indeed seen the ghostly specter of Elizabeth Herndon for that one brief moment, a glimpse into the past.

Some of the volunteers at New Salem will say that they don't always feel alone when no one else is around and that at times they sense that someone is watching them. Staff that experience this don't seem to be rattled by these weird sensations, citing that if there are old ghosts watching them, they're just there watching over the village and living out their ghostly lives. So, when staff encounter the ghostly specter of Dr. Regnier sitting in an invisible chair on the porch of his home, it's as if he's supposed to be there and bothers no one. One volunteer was working in the home waiting for tourists to come inside when she heard a few men talking just outside. The words were unintelligible, but she could clearly hear two men talking; it didn't sound like a conversation that tourists or staff would be having. She got up from her chair and looked outside but saw no one. A former employee was once walking past the blacksmith shop at the end of the day, so the shop was clearly all closed up. But as he walked by, he clearly heard several familiar and unmistakable sounds of a hammer striking an anvil. Perplexed, he thought it was his mind playing tricks on him since it wasn't uncommon to hear the hammering throughout the day. Who knows?

Phantom sounds of the past seem to be the most common paranormal activity in the park. Workers have been known to hear the sounds of everyday life unfolding in a once prosperous village—the sounds of a broom sweeping a wooden floor, shuffling of boots and boot steps and the clank of kitchen activity. One volunteer was standing alone next to an old water well when she unexpectedly heard what she thought sounded like someone bringing up a bucket of water from the well. The sound was unmistakable to her. But she knew that the well was totally dry and filled in. She shyly retreated away from the old well.

Today, New Salem is still a magical and mystical place more than 180 years later. Visiting the re-created village of pioneer log homes on their original foundations is a step back in time. Anyone sauntering through the old village down the main trail is bound to run into staff and volunteers in period clothes and homespun portraying actual residents of New Salem engaged in their livelihoods. Visitors sometimes are in the right place at the right time to catch a mystical glimpse into the original life at new Salem. For the staff, any old ghosts are right where they are supposed to be, and for them, any brushes with the past are endearing and welcome, especially on a slow, rainy day.

Visitors to the park first thing in the morning are treated to a pioneer village waking up for the day—stoked fires in the stone fireplaces giving warmth against the morning chill, the forest coming alive with the sounds of songbirds and dew sparkling off the grass in the sunlight. The smell of the forest. The fresh and clean country air. A visit to New Salem today offers the same spirit of New Salem experienced by the villagers themselves in their time.

# Abraham Lincoln and His Farewell

Springfield's most well-known ghostly tales are associated with Abraham and Mary Lincoln. His departure from Springfield was overshadowed by death threats and a bizarre dream he had at his home on election night. Subtle comments by Lincoln throughout his life may or may not be a reference to his strange, foreboding dreams.

The day before he left for Washington, Lincoln went down to his office to tie up loose ends with his partner, William Herndon. Upon arrival, Lincoln looked up at the "Lincoln and Herndon" sign swinging from its rusty hinges and asked Herndon to leave it up. He said, "Given our clients to understand that the election of a president makes no change in the firm of Lincoln and Herndon." The men went upstairs to conclude their business, and when finished, they descended the stairs to the street. Lincoln declared, "If I live, I'm coming back sometime, and we'll go on practicing like nothing ever happened." Lincoln explained that the sorrow at parting from his old friend was great and made greater by the irrepressible feeling that he would not come back alive.

"If I live." Already Lincoln was haunted by the notion that he might not return to Springfield alive. Tragically, his fears would prove all too justified. Herndon was troubled by this statement. He tried to argue with Lincoln, but they were interrupted by well-wishers as they reached the street. Lincoln clasped Herndon's hand firmly and disappeared down the street, never to return to his office again.

# THE HAUNTED LINCOLNS

Just four blocks from Lincoln's downtown law office is Lincoln's home, where he lived for seventeen years raising a family. Today, it sits in the center of a four-block national park with thirteen other original historic houses. The park is created to look as it did in 1860, Lincoln's last year as a lawyer. Perhaps events of the historic past of the old neighborhood still play out today for those lucky enough to be in the right place at the right time.

It was dusk and the streetlights had just come on when a tour group left the five benches in front of Lincoln's home and began walking north up the street. Near the end of the street, the tour guide noticed that five people were lagging behind back in the intersection in front of Lincoln's house, and just as he was calling out to them to please catch up, suddenly all five of them abruptly turned and together stepped away from something at the same time. Thinking that something had just happened, the guide walked back to the five, and every one of them was unnerved and confused by something. They were in disbelief. They believed that they had just heard a horse and carriage lumbering up the street right behind them. They even commented on the jingle of the carriage and the definite sounds of the horse's hooves thumping into the dirt street from Lincoln's day, not the crunching sounds of the pebbled street today. They were sure that the carriage was right upon them, so they all immediately turned to step out of the way and to get a look, but all they saw was an empty street.

In Lincoln's day, there would have been at least two dozen horses stabled in the neighborhood. Even today, the phantom smell of horses has been known to waft through the neighborhood at any time during day or evening hours, catching people's attention, especially since no horses are ever seen. On rare occasion, the park has been host to reenactors and their horses, and one afternoon the unmistakable smell of horses caught the attention of park staff. Knowing that no horses were to be in the park that day, staff went searching up and down the street. No horses were found. The streets of Lincoln's neighborhood may be haunted by events of the past still playing out today. But what about Lincoln's home?

There are no known stories of Lincoln haunting his home. But the house just might be haunted by Mary Lincoln. Stories about ghostly sightings of an apparition of a woman about five feet tall wearing a hoop skirt have circulated for years. Mary was five-foot-two and wore hoop skirts, and she would have spent considerable time in the home tending to the needs of her family. Another claim suggests that the ghostly woman seen in a bustled dress is a former caretaker of the Lincoln home after the Lincoln years. Mary would have had more of a connection to the house. If it is Mary, the question then becomes why Mary would be haunting the home. Perhaps not all hauntings result from a tragic or untimely death or unfinished business by the deceased. Some hauntings can occur out of a bond or a love for a place, and perhaps that's what we have going on right here. The happiest days of Mary's life were spent here inside this home of seventeen years. Even though Eddie died in this house in 1850, Robert was raised here, and Tad and Willie were born in this house, making for quite cherished memories. Mary was very popular here in Springfield, and her husband was a rising political star. Mary's life was in a downward spiral once the Lincolns left for Washington. There's no doubt that Mary's happiest days of her life were spent here, inside this home, and perhaps in death here she able to relive those happiest of days of her life.

But there is another possible Mary story here. It's been reported usually by tourists in the park at night, standing before the house to take pictures of the house under the ambiance of the old streetlights. While standing there in awe of Lincoln's home, suddenly the lower half of the window to the left of the front door goes dark, as if someone is standing in the window looking out. The dark, shapely figure is gone in just a moment. Witnesses are quick to question what or if they just saw something. But some people who have encountered this say they believe it was Mary Lincoln briefly looking out the window, waiting for her beloved husband to come home from riding the circuit late at night. Lincoln was gone two to three months at a time as a circuit rider, and Mary had to have spent some lonely nights. She must have been curious after a few months had gone by if he was coming home soon.

However, it was also in this house that Lincoln had at least two strange and foreboding dreams. Perhaps dreams of death. On February 1, 1850, Lincoln's second-born son, Eddie, died inside the home. He was approaching his fourth birthday. Later in life, Lincoln commented that he had a perplexing dream the night before Eddie died. He dreamed that he was on a rudderless ship lost at sea, with no particular direction and no port of call to sail to. For Lincoln, this would become a recurring dream during his White House years.

Lincoln had a second dream inside the Springfield home. This one was one of his most bizarre dreams. It came on election night, November 6, 1860. Springfield celebrated big time; there were fireworks and signal cannon fire into the night. It wasn't until late into the night that Lincoln broke away from the celebrations and returned home. Once at home, he

The Lincoln home, decorated in funeral bunting and evergreens for Lincoln's funeral, May 3–4, 1865. *Sangamon Valley Collection.*

retired to his bedroom and laid back on a couch. He could see his round shaving mirror up on the wall. Suddenly, he saw a strange vision inside the mirror, but unsure what he was seeing, a pragmatic Lincoln would have tried to explain it away, perhaps thinking that his eyes were playing tricks on him. Moments later, the vision in the mirror reappeared, but this time it was clearer. Lincoln could now see the silhouette image of two faces. It was his face, but the faces were just opposite of each other, almost touching nose to nose. What struck him odd about the vision was that one face had a normal, healthy skin tone color. But the other face was a pale ash gray— perhaps the color of death came to his mind. The next morning, he told Mary about the vision, and she believed that the two faces inside the mirror represented Lincoln being elected a first and second term as president, but the grayish-looking face perhaps meant that he would not survive his second term. Lincoln openly spoke several times about this foreshadowing dream during his White House years.

Few handwritten acknowledgments of Lincoln's visions and dreams exist, but Lincoln was well known to have open conversation about his bizarre dreams with Mary and close friends such as Ward Hill Lamon and Bill Herndon. They, in turn, wrote about some of these conversations.

In 1863, Lincoln wrote a letter to Mary, who was in Philadelphia at the time with Tad, who was just ten years old. Lincoln told Mary to "put Tad's pistol away" and that he had an "ugly dream about him." The letter does seem to acknowledge that Lincoln was concerned about his strange and bizarre dreams. Perhaps Lincoln had that rudderless ship dream again, but this time he followed a gut instinct.

In what may be a truly bizarre twist of fate, John Wilkes Booth's mother wrote a poem about her son as a result of a reoccurring dream she was having. In 1838, JWB was just six months old when she wrote:

> *Tiny, innocent, white baby hand,*
> *What force, what power is at your command,*
> *For evil, for good? Be slow, or be sure,*
> *Firm to resist, to pure to endure*
> *My God, let me see what this hand will do,*
> *In the silent years we are attending to;*
> *In my lingering Love, I implore to know on this ghostly night,*
> *Whether twill labour for wrong, or right,*
> *For—or against Thee?*

## THE LINCOLNS AND SPIRITUALISM

By the time the Lincolns arrived in Washington, Spiritualism had become the fashionable and in vogue thing to do for the social elite of Washington. It was socially acceptable because a component of Christianity accompanied it. Spiritualism is the practice of communicating with the dead via the use of a psychic medium, who functions as the liaison between the dead and living world. People became fascinated by the profound abilities of psychics who could communicate with dead loved ones to reveal insights into the future and pass messages back and forth between the living and spirit world. But the notion of being able to communicate with their deceased son would have certainly piqued the interest of both of the Lincolns since they were both superstitious growing up.

This was the result of the times and circumstances in which they were living. Abraham and Mary were both superstitious people, but from different backgrounds. A young Lincoln grew up with the known folklore superstitions of early pioneer life in the early 1800s, such as throwing salt over the shoulder to avoid bad luck, burning an even number of candles in the cabin verses an odd number, snuffing candles versus blowing out the candles (spilling wax), covering any mirrors in the cabin upon someone's death and so on. There would have been other superstitions to follow. When Lincoln was ten years old, he began having bizarre dreams and became interested in dream interpretation. It's no surprise, then, that Lincoln had a superstitious nature as an adult and that the curiosity of the unknown and unexplained would prevail in his adult life, especially considering his own bizarre dreams.

As a young girl, Mary grew up with a completely different type of superstition. There were seventeen Todd children, and there was an enslaved person assigned to attend to each child, totaling seventeen slaves in the household. And each of those slaves came over from Africa and brought with them their tales about African medicine men and shamans, folklore and superstitions, magic and mysticism. A young and impressionable Mary was privy to these stories and subsequently developed an interest in interpreting signs, symbols and omens that would have been prevalent in tribal culture.

Once in the White House, it was Mary who began attending a great many number of séances at the home of a man named Cranston Laurie. He was a well-known and popular Georgetown psychic medium. At one of these séances at the Laurie home, Mary was introduced to another medium. Her name was Nettie Colburn. People called her Miss Nettie. There were plenty of fake mediums and charlatans around, using sneaky parlor tricks to fool people, and certainly some may have tried to take advantage of the Lincolns to garner favor in some way. But sixteen-year-old Miss Nettie was popular, and she seemed to be a genuine psychic. Mary decided to invite Nettie to the White House to do a séance for Abraham Lincoln and introduce him to the Spiritualist movement. Mary held at least eight known séances in the Red Room of the White House. Lincoln attended at least two of those séances. At the first séance Lincoln attended, Nettie went into a trance and summoned the spirits. When she recovered from her trances, she was not aware of what was said or occurred. She came out of her trance and saw the president in a chair directly across from her. Lincoln was sitting back in his chair, his arms folded, focused. After what must have been an uncomfortable pause, Lincoln finally responded to her and said, "My God child, you must possess a most singular gift, it is from God no doubt. Your words are more important than you'll ever know." Nettie had been talking about the Emancipation Proclamation; this was intriguing to Lincoln because this was not yet public knowledge, and even if some of the information had leaked out to the public, how could she have known the fine details of the document? She knew details that Lincoln had discussed with only a few of his cabinet members at best. So, for Lincoln, it wasn't plausible that she had the information, let alone the finer details of the text. But she also told Lincoln to not delay its enforcement. She urged him to stand firm on his convictions to see it through and that it would become the crowning achievement of his life. Now, we'll never really know, but perhaps Lincoln took this advice to heart. Despite the fact that his cabinet members were initially against it, he most certainly did sign the Emancipation Proclamation on January 1, 1863.

Lincoln was no doubt intrigued by Miss Nettie's skills, and they developed a friendship. She was invited into the White House on numerous occasions. Unfortunately, there are only minimal references to these visits, and we'll likely never know the full extent of these visits and the conversations that took place.

It was Nettie who consoled the Lincolns in 1862 when an eleven-year-old member of the family passed away in the White House. This death was exceptionally hard on the Lincolns, as they had already lost one child. Mary's grief was so out of control that Lincoln told her she might have to be sent away to an asylum (here a reference to a hospital during this era). Mary did work through her grief, but she also claimed that the ghostly apparition of Willie appeared at the foot of her bed each and every night for several weeks. Some nights he would bring a smiling dear little Eddie. This no doubt provided Mary comfort, letting her know that her children had crossed over into the light of God, that her children were okay and that she could continue on. Perhaps this helped Mary work through her immense loss and grief.

But Lincoln didn't fare any better. He locked himself away in his cabinet room for several days. On the third day, Salmon Chase entered the cabinet room to check on the president. He found Lincoln sitting behind a desk. On top of the desk were toys that Willie had played with just days before. Lincoln stood up, looked down at his side and said, "Do you ever find yourself talking to the dead? I strangely find myself talking to Willie as if he's standing right next to me this very moment." Perhaps Lincoln was not seeing the ghostly apparition of his deceased child like Mary was; perhaps Lincoln was feeling the presence of his deceased child. Perhaps this is how Lincoln worked through his own grief.

In February 1872, Mary Lincoln sat for this photograph in the studio of William Mumler. It shows a ghostly Lincoln standing behind Mary. The photograph was proven to be faked, but Mary always believed that her beloved Abraham was always with her. *Abraham Lincoln Presidential Library.*

But the last meeting that took place between Nettie and Lincoln happened just three weeks before his assassination. Lincoln had a particular battle plan in mind, but he wanted some assurance that he had developed a winning plan, as the Union had been taking some heavy losses. He summoned two military advisors into his cabinet room and shared his idea with his officers. He then summoned Nettie into the room and watched her go into a trance. When she came out of it, she found herself standing before a large battle map up on the wall and holding a pencil in her hand. Lincoln stated, "It is astonishing! Every line she has drawn conforms to the plan we've agreed upon!" This confirmed to Lincoln and his officers that he'd devised a winning battle plan. Nettie was quietly escorted out of the cabinet room, but before she closed the door behind her, she turned to the president and gave him an ominous warning: there is grave danger in his future, and he should guard well. But Lincoln responded flippantly, saying that he believed no harm would ever come to him until his work on earth was done and that no power could ever prevent that. Unfortunately, Lincoln was quite wrong, and he was assassinated just three weeks later. Perhaps Lincoln's work on earth was finally done.

## THE FINAL FOREBODING DREAM

On April 1, with only fourteen days left to live, Lincoln was on board the boat *River Queen*, docked in City Point, Virginia, just outside Petersburg on the Appomattox River. Tensions were high for Lincoln as he awaited General Grant's potential capture of Petersburg. Union guns thundered and pounded away at Confederate defenses into the night. When the guns went silent for the night, a tired and a weary Lincoln finally retreated to his cabin and fell into a deep sleep. He began to experience his most foreboding dream yet. This one troubled Lincoln, and ten days later, once back in Washington, Lincoln recounted the ominous dream to Mary and his best friend and bodyguard, Ward Lamon. He also wrote it down. Lincoln is believed to have said:

> *About ten days ago, I retired late, I soon began to dream. There seemed to be a death like stillness about me. And then I heard subdued sobs as if a number of people were weeping. I thought I left my bed and wandered downstairs. And there the same pitiful sobbing broke the silence, but the*

*mourners were invisible. I went from room to room, no living person was in sight, but the same mournful sounds of distress met me as I passed along. It was light in all the rooms, every object was familiar to me, but where were all those people who were grieving as if their hearts would break? I was puzzled and alarmed. What could be the meaning of this? And determined to find the cause of a state of things so mysterious and shocking I kept on until I arrived at the East Room which I entered. Before me was a catafalque on which rested a corpse wrapped in funeral vestments, around it was stationed as soldiers, they were acting as guards. But there was a throng of people, some gazing mournfully upon the corpse whose face was covered, others were weeping pitifully. Who is dead in the WH I asked of one of the soldiers? The president was his answer. He was killed by an assassin. And then came a loud burst of grief from the crowd which awoke me from my dream! And although it was only a dream, I slept no more that night....I've been strangely annoyed by it ever since.*

On the afternoon of April 14, with only hours left before the assassination, Lincoln held his final cabinet meeting, which lasted nearly four hours. At the outset of that cabinet meeting, he spoke about a dream he had just the night before. He spoke about being on the deck of a mysterious ghost ship, how it was adrift at sea, unable to find any port of call to sail to. It was a familiar dream for Lincoln, a dream that accompanied the president's slumber the night before his son Eddie passed away. He said that he also had the same dream the night before Willie passed away. Lincoln said he had this dream the night before the Union lost several major Civil War battles, and this is also the dream the president had the night before he was assassinated. It would have been Lincoln's last prophetic vision, and it certainly came true.

Did Abraham Lincoln have any idea that this dream of death he had by then become so familiar with would predict his *own* death? We'll never know.

## THE GHOSTLY LINCOLN SPECIAL

Abraham Lincoln's nine-car funeral train, called the Lincoln Special, carried the remains of Abraham and Willie Lincoln from Washington back to Springfield, Illinois. The train never traveled more than twenty miles per hour for the sake of dignity. It was twenty-one days from death until burial for Lincoln.

The Lincoln Special pulled into Springfield, Illinois, around 8:00 a.m. on the morning of May 3, 1865, on the 3rd Street rail line west side tracks. When the train arrived, there were tens of thousands of people not only tightly crowded around the depot but also filling the rooftops of buildings surrounding the depot. Willie's coffin was taken straight out to Oak Ridge Cemetery and placed into the public receiving vault awaiting his father's arrival the following day. Lincoln's coffin was taken to the state capitol and placed in the Illinois House of Representatives for his final farewell.

There are numbers of ghost train stories in American folklore, and the Lincoln Special would find its way into the same legendary status. Stories of encounters with the Lincoln Special still making its annual journey occasionally surface to this day.

But the earliest circulated story found was just months after the Lincoln Special made its run through Philadelphia. It seemed that a lone railroad watchman out in the countryside walking the rails and checking the tracks one summer night took notice of the soft, cool breeze that kicked up. The air pressure changed, becoming heavy and palpable. He noticed

Old Nashville, one of the locomotives that pulled the Lincoln Special. *Library of Congress.*

The funeral car that carried the coffins of Abraham and Willie Lincoln from Washington to Springfield. *Library of Congress.*

a faint single light on the track line miles off in the distance. Knowing that no train was due to be on the tracks at that time, the watchman was perplexed. He continued to walk the tracks, but just moments later, the wind kicked up stronger. He looked up. Astonished, he saw that the light on the tracks was suddenly closer and closing in on him. He recognized the search light on the front of a locomotive. He knew the Lincoln Special had run right down these very tracks just months ago, and he now sensed that something astounding was about to happen. Thinking that he should get off the tracks, the watchman sat down in the grass next to the tracks. Moments later, a powerful swirling wind roared down the tracks, and suddenly a steam locomotive appeared, thundering and chugging, with burning embers billowing from the smokestack! There was a picture of Lincoln secured above the cowcatcher, so it had to be the Lincoln Special. The train was speeding and roaring by, pulling multiple cars, but a moment of time seemed to pause just long enough for the watchman to see Lincoln's funeral car with his coffin surrounded by soldiers. A moment later, it was gone. The entire episode lasted only a few seconds. The night went silent, and the tracks were empty once again. A gentle, cool summer breeze returned to the night. The watchman took a great pause at what had just happened and realized that he had witnessed a spectral train, the ghostly Lincoln Special, the sort of thing legends are made of.

There are some who believe that the ghostly Lincoln Special still makes its annual journey, bringing the president home each year. There's a neighborhood in south Indianapolis where the Lincoln Special once ran the tracks in 1865. Residents have talked about the phantom train still traveling through the neighborhood each year. The unique sound of a steam whistle can be repeatedly heard for several minutes coinciding with the time the historic train came through. Witnesses say that the whistle is faint at first but is followed by a few slightly louder blasts before fading into the night. Some residents even report the phantom smells of burning coal. The event is over in moments.

## Skullduggery at the Lincoln Tomb

Lincoln's funeral procession entered the cemetery and stopped in front of the receiving vault. Lincoln's coffin was placed inside next to Willie's, the doors were closed and locked and sentries were posted to stand guard. Within a few days of Lincoln's interment in the vault, though, mourners out at the cemetery had begun to report sightings of Lincoln's ghostly apparition patrolling the hillside above where his tomb would later be built. This began to foster a superstitious belief with the public that Lincoln was not resting in peace and that if he was seen posthumously wandering the hillside, it meant he could not be inside his coffin at all. People were more superstitious in 1865.

Seven months later, with the approach of winter in December, the space inside the vault was needed for winter burials. Both coffins were moved from the receiving vault up to a temporary hillside crypt halfway up the hill. But at this time, seven friends of Lincoln's, perhaps spurred on by the ghostly sightings, decided to open his coffin for the first time, simply to verify that Lincoln's remains were inside.

They called on Leon Hopkins, a plumber's assistant, who went to the cemetery and cut out a small square opening in the top of Lincoln's five-hundred-pound lead-lined coffin. The men peered in and verified that Lincoln was present. Eddie was moved from another cemetery, and now Eddie, Willie and Lincoln were resting in the hillside crypt.

In July 1871, the three coffins were moved up to the tomb site on top of the hill from the hillside crypt. Tad had passed away from TB, and he was also placed in the tomb. The tomb was not complete, but it could receive the Lincolns in Memorial Hall, the burial chamber within. Before Lincoln was placed inside the tomb, those same friends opened his coffin a second time, presumably in another effort to prove to the public that Lincoln was inside. The public still did not believe that he was in there. After verification, the coffin was interred inside the tomb and construction continued. But the workmen began to speak of strange things happening at the tomb. Phantom footsteps were said to be heard pacing across the tiled floors, while other men spoke of a doleful weeping sound that echoed throughout the catacomb. Despite the ghostly happenings, the work continued. By 1874, the tomb had been completed.

Lincoln's coffin was to be placed in a white marble sarcophagus. The tomb was opened to the public the following day. But before placing his coffin into the sarcophagus, those friends of Lincoln opened the coffin a third time. Again, Lincoln was right where he should be, and the coffin was placed into the sarcophagus. The tomb was then opened to the public. However, the public began reporting the same phantom footsteps and the same doleful weeping sounds. Many people believed that they encountered Lincoln's ghostly specter wandering the grounds surrounding the tomb, perpetuating the belief that he's still searching for his final resting place.

In that era, it was feared that someone would try to desecrate the tomb in some way. After all, there were plenty of Confederate sympathizers still about. In 1876, such fears of skullduggery at the tomb came true! A band of counterfeiters tried to break into the tomb to steal Lincoln's body and hold it for ransom.

These men had Lincoln's coffin pulled about one foot outside of the sarcophagus when Pinkerton detectives and Secret Service agents, who had infiltrated the gang, attempted to arrest the men. A sensational shootout began in the back doorway of the tomb, with the sounds of the heated gun battle echoing throughout the back of the cemetery and down the hill behind the tomb. Things became confusing in the dark and the criminals escaped. They were captured ten days later, but they were all given only one-year sentences in the Joliet State Penitentiary.

There was nothing illegal in 1876 Illinois about digging up bodies in cemeteries. You could have dug up all the bodies you wanted then. They received that year in prison for simply cutting a padlock off the back door of the tomb, destroying state property.

John Power, the curator of the tomb, was terrified that something like that might happen again. So, he and one of the marble workers dragged Lincoln's coffin into a rear labyrinth of the tomb and began to dig a new grave for the president. But as they worked into the night, water seeped into the grave, collapsing the walls. They were unable to dig a proper grave, as it quickly filled up with muddy, murky water. They were not about to bury the president in an undignified grave such as this, but they were running out of time, as the public would be showing up soon. So, they gave up and simply covered the president's coffin with a pile of boards and rubble left over from the construction of the tomb. For the next year, visiting mourners to the tomb paid their respects to an empty sarcophagus.

In 1877, the addition of the military statues on the tomb would take workers into the chamber where Lincoln's coffin was located under the rubble. It was decided to tell the workers about Lincoln's hidden coffin and swear them to secrecy. However, by the next day, the scandal was out to the public, perpetuating the belief that Lincoln was not in his coffin since his coffin was not where it was supposed to be. The public felt lied to and betrayed, ever doubtful of information. In the wake of the scandal, Lincoln was pulled out from under the pile of boards and rubble, taken to another part of the tomb and reburied in a very shallow grave. He would remain there for a number of years, and the public would unknowingly continue to pay their respects to an empty sarcophagus for years to come.

On July 16, 1882, Mary Lincoln passed away. After her funeral, Robert requested that his mother be secretly hidden away with his father. So, under the cover of night, without the public or the press having any knowledge, John Power enlisted the help of those friends of Lincoln. The eight men carried Mary's coffin into the same rear labyrinth where Lincoln lay in that shallow grave.

Finally, by 1886, the Lincolns had been placed into a new crypt and what should have been the final burial for the Lincolns. But first those friends of Lincoln opened his coffin for the fourth time, what would have been the last time, to prove he was in the coffin. Of course, he was there. The boys would remain in their sarcophagi for now, and both Mary and Abraham were interred in the crypt. It was over at last.

Unfortunately, something catastrophic happened in 1899. The tomb cracked due to uneven settlement. The government had no choice but to tear down the entire tomb and start over. But what to do with the Lincoln coffins? They were all deceased except for Robert. So, a mass grave was dug just behind the tomb. The Lincoln family were placed into the mass grave, and as the tomb was torn down, slabs of rubble were placed over the grave to protect the Lincolns from any would-be grave robbers.

By 1901, the new tomb had been completed and was ready to receive what would surely be the final burial for the Lincolns. Robert was still concerned about another attempt on his father's coffin, so he requested

The Lincoln family tomb, where Abraham, Mary, Eddie, Willie and Tad Lincoln are interred. Robert Lincoln and his family are buried at Arlington National Cemetery. *Garret Moffett.*

that his mother and brothers be placed inside the wall crypts and that his father be buried in a grave of ten feet, versus the standard six feet. He also wanted the grave lined with a steel cage. Once his father's coffin was lowered in, he wanted ten tons of concrete poured over the coffin, encasing his father in a crypt of concrete. Well, considering the permanency of this type of a burial, those friends of Lincoln decided to open the coffin for the fifth time, in what was to be the final viewing of Lincoln in 1901.

These men set up Lincoln's coffin on a set of sawhorses in a dimly lit burial chamber. They lifted away that square opening, soon to be the last time the men were overcome by the sweet stench of rotting corpse. But the men were amazed to see how remarkably well-preserved Lincoln was in 1901. In fact, he was perfectly recognizable. The only noted deterioration was that his skin had fully darkened, and his eyebrows had fallen away. They noted that the headrest of the coffin had given way, so Lincoln's head was now hyper-extended back. Most notably was our American flag. It was still clutched in Lincoln's lifeless hands, but the flag was now faded and shredded. Old Glory was in tatters. But it is Abraham Lincoln after all, about to be placed right where he should be. Lincoln was lowered down into the crypt, and the concrete was poured over, encasing Lincoln in a crypt of concrete—belonging to the ages, for all ages to come.

## Oak Ridge Cemetery's Receiving Vault

The vault can be found behind the Lincoln Tomb at the bottom of the hill. These type of vaults were a necessity of the 1800s because there was no way to dig graves during winter's frozen ground. Bodies were stored in the public receiving vault until the spring thaw, when graves could be dug again. Vaults such as this one fell out of use once steam-powered mechanical equipment came into use.

When Lincoln's funeral train returned to Springfield, Lincoln's body was taken to the state capitol for a twenty-four-hour repose period. Willie's remains were taken straight out to Oak Ridge Cemetery from the train station and placed inside the receiving vault awaiting his father's arrival the next day.

Early afternoon on May 4, Lincoln's funeral procession entered the main gate of the cemetery, which is the white archway to the east of the public receiving vault. Nearly 12,000 people were sitting on the hillside all around the receiving vault. The opposing hill and ridge line to the north of the vault was devoid of trees in 1865, where another 100,000 people watching Lincoln's interment into the vault.

After a two-hour benediction in high humidity, the gates of the vault were locked. It was finally over for the fallen president.

Between May and December 1865, nine soldiers were assigned to stand guard over Abraham and Willie Lincoln. One of those soldiers said in his diary that standing a post guarding Lincoln was his greatest honor in life. No doubt any soldier given such a task would experience a personal sense of pride and importance to be given such a task. Lincoln certainly had enemies; the gates of the vault were locked only by a single paddle lock, and both coffins were visible. Guards were needed until Lincoln's remains could be better secured from anyone with nefarious intentions.

Emotional events in history are known to still play out today through paranormal events like a video that loops and plays over and over. Lincoln's funeral was the first of its kind in America—the first president murdered—and it took an emotional toll on anyone who had affections for Lincoln. Think of those soldiers who were assigned to stand a post guarding over the Lincolns. It had to be a mixture of sadness and pride while remaining vigilant for anyone seeking to disrespect the fallen president.

Today, people like to stop and visit the old receiving vault to peer in and ponder the Lincoln funeral history that once unfolded right here. Occasionally, people standing there with family or friends claim to have heard a very soft voice say "Ma'am" or "Excuse me, ma'am" and turn to look but see no one else around. Others have stated that they've heard the murmur of faint unintelligible voices, thinking that other people were walking up to the vault, but again no one else is seen.

But there's one unnerving encounter that seems to play over and over, as it's been reported several times. Prior to 2014, the flanking stone walls on either side of the vault were badly crumbling and in need of repair. Unscrupulous people were known to take pieces of the crumbing wall with them as souvenirs, which of course is very disrespectful.

In one instance, a woman was visiting the vault by herself, peering in and no doubt intrigued by the history. She said that she revered Abraham Lincoln and had hoped that during her Springfield visit she could connect to Lincoln in her own way. That's when she noticed that the wall was crumbling and that there were loose pieces of the wall everywhere. Hesitating at first, she looked around carefully and swore that there was not another person in sight. She was by herself standing there at the vault. She reached out, pulled

Soldiers guarding over Abraham and Willie Lincoln inside the old receiving vault before the tomb was built, May 1865. *Library of Congress.*

out a piece of the wall and dropped it into her pocket. All of a sudden, without question, she heard distinctive heavy footsteps running right up behind her! Alarmed, she thought she had just been caught red-handed, and without turning around to look, she pulled the piece of the wall out of her pocket and immediately dropped it on the sidewalk. She turned around thinking that she was about to be admonished, but there was no one else there. Her chest pounded. Not a person was in sight, but to her the boot steps were unmistakable.

Standing there alone, she took a moment to digest what had just happened. She was adamant about the footsteps that she heard. She decided not to pick up the piece of wall she had dropped, feeling guilty. She realized she had indeed made her own connection to Lincoln by experiencing a moment in history, perhaps with a soldier still standing his post guarding over the Lincolns.

It's interesting that a number of these bizarre soldier encounters were reported in 2014–15, when the receiving vault was finally restored. In 2015, the Lincoln funeral reenactment took place, where a reproduction coffin was placed inside the vault and guards stood a post once again.

Abraham Lincoln is no doubt Springfield's most famous and legendary figure, and an entire volume could be dedicated to the subject and the attendant ghost stories. But there's a number of other ghostly stories woven into the fabric of Springfield's haunted history too.

# THE FATEFUL DONNER PARTY

Springfield is known for Abraham Lincoln and its unique pioneer history, but there is a faded, yet bizarre, story associated with Springfield concerning the "Fateful Donner Party of 1846." It is a story that exemplifies the ultimate act of survival, one that is difficult for any one of us to comprehend in today's world. Although it is not a typical ghost story in the paranormal sense, there is no doubt that the survivors were haunted every day for the rest of their lives—haunted by the memories of what they endured that winter of 1846.

California and Oregon Territories were unsettled lands to Americans in the 1840s. Those tempted by the abundant land, bountiful game and the opportunity to own their own land joined wagon trains headed west. The pilgrimage itself was to cleanse the past—to settle in a new land and start a new life had become the American dream. It was attainable for anyone willing to take on the challenge and danger of Mother Nature and make the treacherous journey across an unforgiving land, vast plains and a looming mountain range. Nineteen years before President Lincoln's death on April 15, 1846, George Donner and James Reed, along with their families and hired hands, totaling thirty-three people on board a dozen wagons pulled by oxen, departed Springfield, Illinois, from what is known as the Old State Capitol Plaza.

Westward bound, the Donners' wagon train joined up with other wagons also headed west, and the train grew to nearly two hundred people and three dozen wagons. They followed the California Trail until they reached the

Little Sandy River in Wyoming and set up camp. At this point, the migrants became divided over which trail to proceed on. Some wanted to travel the northern route through the mountain passes. It would take longer, but it was a known route and considered safe enough. Others, believing that the supplies might not hold out on the longer route, were vying for a shorter, lesser-known route through the mountains. Overshadowing their decision was the fact that supplies were already low, and winter would be arriving soon. Regardless of which route they chose, the migrants had to make it through the mountain passes before winter set in or they would risk getting trapped there by snow.

Complicating the matter for those wanting to take the shorter route, they would have to catch up to Landsford Hastings, who was just ahead of them, guiding his own wagon train. He knew the shorter route, and George Donner argued that they could make haste and catch Hastings. There would be safety in numbers crossing through the mountains and reaching their destination before supplies ran out.

However, unable to agree on which route to take, the group split into two separate wagon trains. One wagon train headed for the northern but longer route, and the remaining eighty making up the Donner party headed south to catch up with Hastings.

As the Donner party trudged along, the wagon train was belabored by problems and setbacks, causing significant delays. The trail was barely passible in some places; wagons had mechanical problems and accidents, and hills were steep, making it difficult for the oxen to pull the heavily laden wagons. By now, they had traveled one thousand miles and were not far from their final destination. They had endured great hardship on the trail, but their greatest test and worst fears were yet to come. When they finally reached the Nevada-Sierra Mountains at the end of October, they had to face the harsh reality that the so-called shorter route had taken them three weeks longer than expected. Hastings's wagons had already left their base camp and were headed on through the mountains. Hastings could wait no longer for the Donner party to arrive. He had to get his own wagon train through the mountains before winter set in.

Supplies were now dangerously low, and the Donners were demoralized. To set up a winter camp where they were would force them to live off the land and could mean starvation. The supplies would quickly run out, and adding to their frustration was the fact that they were within one hundred miles of Sutter's Fort on the other side of the mountains, where shelter and supplies would be available to them.

Because of the three-week delay, the only real choice was to push on and get through the mountain passes before the snow arrived. If they failed, it would mean certain death.

The Donner party pressed forward through the mountains, but the migrants were met by an early winter storm that blocked the mountain pass just ahead. This would be the death knell for the Donner party.

Now the grim reality of having to survive a winter trapped in the mountains was becoming clear. Pushing on through the pass was impossible. They had to suspect at this point that many of them would not survive. The migrants decided to hunker down and dig in for the winter, as it seemed to be the best hope for survival. They set camp at what is known today as Donner Lake, but survival instincts kicked in and some of them wanted to push forward rather than face certain death. One-third of the wagons pushed on, but they made it only six miles down the snow-covered trail before they realized that their efforts were futile. The snow was too deep to walk through, let alone oxen trying to pull heavy wagons through. They set camp at Adler Creek.

Migrants at both camps could build only crude shelters that were more like lean-tos. It takes considerable time to build a cabin that will endure Mother Nature. They had few supplies to work with, and the snow was deep, making it difficult to cut and move heavy timbers. The winter's bitter cold made spending time out in the elements difficult with the limited clothing they possessed. Furthermore, they were demoralized, and teamwork was impossible. Instead of banding together in a large group for survival, they huddled together in small groups, seemingly only concerned for their own survival.

By now it was mid-December, and spring was still three months away. With the food all gone, they had no choice but to slaughter the oxen, but it would not be enough to feed so many for very long. By now, all of the wildlife had settled down or hibernated for the winter, and the migrants knew that they would face a horrific death by starvation if food could not be obtained.

A band of fifteen men led by James Reed decided to make the less than one-hundred-mile trek to Sutter's Fort on makeshift snowshoes to get help. The survival of the camp depended on the success of their arduous journey through the deep snow. The men were named the "Forlorn Hope," as their chances of reaching Sutter's Fort were pitiful. Yet without their success, there would be only one remaining survival option for the starving migrants: cannibalizing the dead.

On the treacherous hike through the winter elements, one man gave out and had to be left behind, certain to die of exposure. The fourteen remaining members of the Forlorn Hope soon became lost in the mountains, and they ran out of food. Starving, cold and caught in a blizzard without shelter, four more men quickly succumbed to the elements and died. It would be impossible to continue on without food, and there was no point in turning back. The remaining ten men had no choice but to eat the frozen and raw flesh of the four dead men in order to survive and continue on. Three more soon died, and their bodies were cannibalized as well. Barely alive, the surviving seven men of the Forlorn Hope arrived at Sutter's Fort, now Sacramento, on the western side of the mountains, on January 18, 1847.

Between February and April, four different rescue parties set out from Sutter's Fort to rescue the trapped and starving settlers. When the first rescue party arrived at the lake camp, they found fourteen dead settlers, the remaining twenty extremely weak. They had been surviving by eating the last of the boiled ox hide.

The second rescue party arrived one week later at the creek-side camp, where rescuers were horrified to find skeletal remains in some of the crude cabins. Their bodies had been cannibalized by the fourteen settlers, now rescued.

The third rescue party returned with only four migrants, and by the time the fourth rescue party arrived, only one man remained alive. The last surviving Donner party member arrived at Sutter's Fort on April 29, 1847, just one year after their westward departure in Springfield, Illinois.

Of the original eighty members of the Donner party, forty-four had survived by eating the flesh of the thirty-six dead. They would live on, but any hardships they faced as they aged would be nothing compared to their harrowing experience in the mountains.

Unfortunately, as if their personal demons weren't enough, the survivors had to endure years of criticism by the public. They were accused of murder and inhumane conduct, although no formal charges were ever brought forth.

George Donner and his wife did not survive, although all of their children did. James Reed's family were one of two families who did not suffer any losses, but James Reed took the blame for the demise of the Donner party.

Today, the campsites at Donner Lake and Adler Creek are National Historic Landmarks.

The story is horrifying to tell, but to live through it is even harder for us to comprehend. Imagine these migrants trapped in the snowy mountains,

A sketch depicting the harsh, brutal and unforgiving conditions that the Donner party faced once the winter's snow arrived, trapping the settlers in the mountains. *Public domain.*

living in crude makeshift shelters with no real food for months. When the last of the food was gone, the only option for survival was to turn to the bodies of the dead.

Eliza Donner later wrote in her diary:

*It had been snowing for three days, and darkness came and somehow they managed to light a fire. They had been three days without food of any kind and most of them were far gone. Even in their delirium they knew they were dying.*

*Even the wind seemed to hold its breath as the suggestion was made that were one to die, the rest might live. Then the suggestion was made that lots be cast and whoever drew the longest slip should be the sacrifice. The slips of paper were prepared, and it was Patrick Dolan that drew the fatal slip. No one had the heart to kill him.*

*About 11:00 o'clock, the storm had increased to a perfect tornado and in an instant blew away every spark of fire. The company was now engaged in imploring God for mercy and relief. That night's bitter cries, anguish and despair never can be forgotten. Somehow William Eddy got his dying companions to sit together in a ring and pull blankets over them. A canopy of snow quickly covered the starving group. Antonio, a Mexican teamster died. Franklin Graves was next. He died in the arms of his daughters Mary and Sarah. Patrick Dolan went insane and had to be held down by his companions. At last, he slipped into a coma and died. Twelve-year-old Lem Murphy lay shuddering, all but dead. It stopped snowing. William Eddy crawled out of his white tomb where dead and dying lay and managed to light a fire. Someone cut the flesh from the arms and legs of Patrick Dolan. They roasted the meat and ate it, averting their faces from each other and weeping. The remaining flesh was butchered, wrapped, and carefully labeled so no one had to eat their kin. Three days later the food was gone and talk of murdering for food became talk in the camp. We looked at each other with suspicion and we withdrew from each other. It was no longer helping each other to survive, it was now only the strong survive. We were all going insane.*

# SPRINGFIELD'S DR. FRANKENSTEIN

There have been seven hangings in Sangamon County between 1826 and 1927—each person convicted of murder. The gallows are long gone, but several of the early hangings took place in an area somewhere between the south wing of the state capitol building and the Illinois State Museum. Later hangings took place in the Sangamon County jail yard at the corner of 7th and Jefferson. But it was the early hanging of Nathaniel Van Noy on November 26, 1826, that would create and give life to Springfield's Dr. Frankenstein story. It was the first hanging in the county.

Van Noy was convicted of murdering his wife in a fit of drunken rage and sentenced to death by the rope. While waiting in his jail cell for his death day, Van Noy summoned a Dr. Phyllio to come see him. Van Noy wanted to know if he could be brought back to life after his hanging with the use of "batteries" that had been recently invented. The doctor surmised that if his neck wasn't broken and the batteries were strong enough, they might work. For a price, the men made a deal. If the experiment in the reanimation of dead tissue didn't work, then the doctor could have his body for medical dissection. Bodies for dissection were hard to come by for doctors, and either way, no matter the outcome, the doctor would be paid. He's either made famous by bringing a dead man back to life or he gets a free human body for dissection.

On the day of the hanging, a shackled Van Noy rode in the back of a wagon from the jail downtown to the execution site in a field just south of the current capitol building. Everyone in the county came out to see the spectacle of a hanging. The streets were lined with the curious and hecklers, with some folks jeering at Van Noy. Others threw rotten vegetables at him as he rode by. Despite the haranguing by gawkers, it's noted that Van Noy kept a calm demeanor, singing hymns and reciting Bible passages, seemingly accepting of his impending death.

The wagon arrived at the primitive gallows, which were nothing more than two upright posts with a single crossbeam connecting them. The wagon was driven between the posts, where a hanging rope was placed around Van Noy's neck, and then the wagon was unceremoniously pulled forward, causing Van Noy to dangle and hang. However, the sheriff sensed that something was afoot with the doctor and insisted that Van Noy hang for a full hour before being taken down.

Dr. Phyllio took charge of Van Noy's body and took him to his medical office located just a few blocks away in downtown Springfield. The doctor then attached several different electrodes from a set of galvanic batteries to various points across the chest of the corpse in an attempt to restart the heart. The doctor was hopeful because the neck had not been broken, but an hour had gone by and rigor was setting in. The public, curious as to what the doctor was up to, lined up outside his office windows by the dozens hoping to catch a glimpse of the morbid experiment. The doctor fired up the batteries, and almost immediately the doctor was stunned to see muscle twitches across Van Noy's chest. Could this be happening for real, the reanimation of dead tissue? The possibility of success was dashed, as the batteries were only strong enough to produce muscle twitches—nowhere near strong enough to defibrillate the heart back into an electric rhythm. The moment was over. The experiment was not a success.

Corpses begin to decay right away upon death, and with more than an hour gone by and the experiment a failure, Dr. Phyllio then began the immediate medical dissection of the body. Members of the public, still staring through the windows of his doctor's office, were horrified to be witness to the dissection. Some people turned away in disgust, and others tried to put a stop to the dissection, citing its cruelty. The procedure continued in a back room out of public view after it was established that the doctor had legal rights to the corpse per his arrangement.

Dr. Phyllio, Springfield's Dr. Frankenstein, likely had no idea that he was somewhat on the right track using electrical conductivity to restart the heart, known today as defibrillation of the heart or shocking the heart back into a normal rhythm.

# THE GIBSON GIRL HAUNTING OF LAWRENCE HOUSE

Springfield socialite Susan Lawrence Dana inherited a large sum of money when her father died, and perhaps hoping to honor her father's legacy, she had an extravagant home designed and built by famed architect Frank Lloyd Wright. This home could be the site of Springfield's most active and credible haunting, as the home is host to more than one spirit. This home can be creepy during the day on a regular home tour, and staff and visitors report ghostly activity at all hours, day or night.

The history of this home is fascinating, and the life story of Susan Lawrence Dana is equally fascinating and complex. It is the story of life on Aristocracy Hill, one of privilege, wealth, world travel and social status but little happiness and plenty of tragedy. Two of her husbands died, and a third marriage ended in divorce. Both of her children died young; one lived only a few hours and the second only two months. Susan was a Gibson Girl of her time. Her eccentric lifestyle tested the boundaries of society. A woman well ahead of her time, she kept her friends and the public guessing about what she might engage in next.

Upon completion of the home in 1904, Susan had a fantastic dinner party for all of the workers who constructed her new home. Subsequently, she began to play host to a number of fantastic and lavish dinner parties that were well attended by other socialites. Susan continued to climb the social ladder in Springfield. She became known for her charitable nature and contributions to causes throughout the city. Susan and her cousin Flora were close; Flora moved into the house upon completion and became Susan's sidekick, so to speak, and an integral part of Susan's social, entertaining and personal life. The house was built for entertaining, and entertain Susan did, receiving guests such as Governor Charles Deneen and even John Philip Sousa.

Spiritualism—consorting with psychics and mediums to communicate with the dead to gain insights into the future—was the new social activity of the day. At this initial dinner party, a local Spiritualist medium suggested that Susan write letters to those she wished to communicate with. The medium instructed her to put the letters in her mailbox and then she would receive letters in reply from those she wrote. Wisdom would come with the responses. Susan wrote to her deceased father a letter: "Papa, do you know about the new home and are you pleased with it? Did I handle your will the way you wanted me to? I did the best I could. Susie."

She received a reply from her deceased father, but it's likely that the reply came from the medium. Letters would simply appear in Susan's mailbox without explanation. "Susie, I love the new house.…I often visit there. You handled the will all right. Lovingly and devoted, Father."

Comforted by the responses and with so much strife in her life, an intrigued Susan then turned to the Spiritualist movement, perhaps seeking further comfort and personal fulfillment. Between 1904 and 1905, she wrote several letters to her dearly departed and received potentially ghostly replies from the other side. Susan soon fully embraced the Spiritualist movement and became a practitioner herself.

In the letters, she asked for insights into her financial future. Although she was an adult, she clearly still sought approval from her departed mother and father, asking "if she was on the right path." She also expressed great loneliness: "I am so lonely…my poor heart aches until I almost die.…God help me, I suffer so." She even signed her letters, "Your little girl, Susie." The "spirit" replies were supportive, touting a higher mission in life for her and offering loving words of comfort, but they seldom gave any real predictions. Susan's letters and the replies were sometimes written on torn paper or envelopes. The handwriting was frequently sloppy and erratic.

Times were certainly good for Susan socially, but a series of family deaths caused her to withdraw from public life briefly. Susan found comfort and solace in her belief that there was more to life after death. She soon returned to throwing lavish parties, but with a new twist. She began to now host numbers of metaphysical meetings and séances in the barrel-vaulted room of her house, which quickly became the center of the Spiritualist movement in Springfield. Her occult parties were well attended, and she soon became a Spiritualist leader. She began to use her astrological name of Zane at her Spiritualist services and meetings.

She practiced her spiritual powers through exercises like slate writing, where the dead send messages in words randomly written on a slate by Susan, now a medium, and speaking in tongues, where the living speak lost languages. Susan's deceased mother wrote to Susan a letter and instructed her to meet her in her old bedroom three times a week to receive wisdom and knowledge. Susan would sit and diligently meditate in her mother's old bedroom, honing her skills faithfully every Monday, Wednesday and Friday, from noon to one o'clock in the afternoon.

Her séances and metaphysical meetings were so well attended that they soon outgrew the home. Susan then moved the séances into one of her downtown properties, where her metaphysical society met with great attendance. The building still stands in the 300 block of south 6th Street and has the name Lawrence at the top of the structure.

Susan and her cousin Flora lived in the house for a number of years, living the life of Riley, only with séances thrown into list of the social activities. Susan and Flora were close, and when Flora died, Susan no doubt felt very alone in the big home. She quickly moved into a smaller cottage next door. In 1942, Susan was declared insane by a court of law and placed in St. John's Hospital. Her personal effects were sold off in 1943 to help pay the mounting debt on the home, and her home was sold off in 1944. Susan, the well-known Gibson Girl, died in 1946.

Today, the well-preserved home is owned and operated by the State of Illinois. It is host to a wide range of paranormal activities that you would expect in a haunted house, but some of the inexplicable ghostly encounters are just amazing.

During a re-creation and reenactment of Susan's mother's Victorian funeral in the barrel-vaulted room of the house, where the séances occurred, the flames of two candles on either side of the coffin kept blowing over in unison, as if a strong breeze had suddenly materialized. No one was seen blowing on the candles, which would have been obvious. The minister was even distracted from his readings by the tipping flames, and people in the audience quietly pointed at the candles as well. After the reenacted funeral, the actors and staff spent time trying to determine just how the candles were being blown on, but no such vents or breezes could be accounted for. It was an unexplainable event that was witnessed by several dozen people

The Dana-Thomas House, built by Frank Lloyd Wright. This is Springfield's house "built by spirits." *Garret Moffett.*

during opening hours of the home. Perhaps it was Susan's way of showing her affection for her mother and that she was present, or maybe she was showing some appreciation for the reenactment?

The home is well alarmed with motion alarms, which are inexplicably tripped occasionally at night in various parts of the home when no one is around. After police investigate, staff will have to show up to reset the alarm, and they sometimes find that something strange has happened within the historic home. One night, the alarm was tripped by a thundering rainstorm. A staff member was there to reset the alarm, but in the dark of the night, with the thunder outside, the staff member paused in front of the main fireplace to admire the unique sound of the rain hitting the roof. Suddenly, the fireplace grate started rattling, shaking and moving on the bricks for several seconds before it stopped. As the rattling stopped, so did the thunder outside, and the staff member was taken aback by the dead silence in the house. The man claimed that he stood there for several more moments, and the grate didn't budge with new claps of thunder. He said he never paid much attention to the stories and had never been unnerved

The Gibson Girl: Susan Lawrence Dana in 1905. *Sangamon Valley Collection.*

in the house before. This time was different for him—he didn't feel alone. He set the alarm and left.

On another night when the alarm tripped, a staff member found things quite amiss in the library. All of the curtains from the hallway were off the windows and piled up in the middle of the floor, except one pair of curtains, which were neatly folded and placed across the back of a chair. The curtain rods were still affixed to the window trim, so in order for someone to remove the curtains from the rods, someone would have to unscrew a number of brackets to slide the curtains off the rods and then reattach all of the rods and brackets. This would have taken a reasonable amount of time even with a screw gun. Why was no one caught in the act when the alarm triggered during this time-consuming ghostly prank?

Sometimes when staff arrive in the mornings for work, they find things in the house askew. The house has perhaps one hundred doors—bedrooms, closets and cabinets—and there's quite a number of small built-in wall cabinets and tucked-away storage compartments, all with little doors. The doors are kept closed for security and fire safety reasons. One morning, an employee came into work and was astonished to find every single door in the

Susan standing outside the front door of her lavish mansion in 1910. The musician's balcony overlooking the living room are the windows just above her. *Sangamon Valley Collection.*

house standing wide open. Unnerved by this weird event, the staff member chose to wait outside the home until other staff members arrived for work that morning before going around and closing all of the doors, together in pairs. It was incredibly unnerving.

Another staff member was in the basement one morning when he heard someone come in the back kitchen door, which has its own separate door alarm. This was odd to him because this door isn't used by tourists, and staff rarely used it—and why had the door alarm not sounded? He briskly went back upstairs to find that no one else was present and the kitchen door was standing wide open.

Other strange things have been known to happen right in front of the eyes of unsuspecting visitors to the home. The home tour once began with seated tourists and a slideshow. One day, the guide was about to start the projector when suddenly there was a very loud crash elsewhere in the house. Startled and concerned, the guide left immediately to investigate but found nothing out of place. By the time he returned to the room, the slideshow had started on its own, but according to the tourists, they said the projector started and skipped through all of the slides but stopped on the very last slide, a picture of Susan Lawrence Dana herself.

Objects that have been misplaced suddenly reappear moments or days later without a plausible explanation. A staff member was cutting ribbon to place across chairs so no one would sit in them. She sat the scissors and the ribbon down and walked away for a moment. When she returned, the ribbon and scissors were gone, yet no one else was in the area. She came back a short while later again only to find that the ribbon was now sitting in the chair right where she left it, but the scissors were stuck in the back of the chair, causing concern for the artifact as well as for the bizarre and unsettling occurrence.

Visitors to the house have mentioned that a shadowy female figure breezes by doors and across halls in the distance. When they ask their plains-clothed guide about seeing the costumed guide, they're told that there are no costumed interpreters in the house—only for special events. Other visitors report the strong smell of cherry tobacco pipe smoke in the kitchen pantry. This was Susan's father's favorite tobacco flavor. Unintelligible voices have also been heard coming from the same pantry unnerving witnesses.

Unintelligible voices in low tones have been heard in other various rooms, and some have reported hearing heavy breathing. Even phantom music has been heard playing from the musician's balcony, which seems to be a fairly active area of the home.

Christmas is a big deal in the home today, and it's decorated with cheerful splendor every year. It is impressive! During the holidays, the home has live musicians performing Christmas music. A dulcimer player claims to have had several bizarre experiences while performing on the musician's balcony. During one open house, he was performing on the balcony and was aware of the warmth of the sun streaming in the windows on such a cold winter day; suddenly, a sharp coldness overcame the area despite the sun radiating in, making it difficult to concentrate and perform. A nearby staff member also became acutely aware of the sudden chill and mentioned that she could feel a cold breeze go through her hair briefly.

The dulcimer player commented that on another occasion when he was playing, his expensive instrument suddenly lost tune in the middle of his performance, which had never happened to him before. He said it was as if someone unseen just reached out and turned the tuning key on the dulcimer. But the most bizarre encounter happened when a tour group passed right by him while performing—three stragglers got his attention, especially one in the long, dark coat. She stood next to him smiling for several moments and watched him play "What Child Is This?" When he was finished, he looked up and noticed that she was gone, but he hadn't seen her walk away. He mentioned the experience with the woman to a staff member, who casually replied, "Oh, you've seen her, haven't you? That's her favorite Christmas song." The staff member was referring to ghostly sightings of a woman thought to be Susan's mother, who has been seen in the balcony area, and paranormal-minded people have repeatedly singled out this area as a hot spot for activity. It believed that the three women were Susan's mother, Flora and Susan herself.

Some of the more common strange occurrences reported by visitors include the feeling of being watched or sensing a presence when no one is seen. The house does have a creepy vibe to it during the day, even when nothing paranormal has been experienced. But the most unnerving presence can sometimes be felt in the basement.

The basement bowling alley is host to unexplained activity. Some people have reported feeling a dark and negative presence in the area. Enough people have sensed this presence that, by this point, they're ready to finish up the tour and get back upstairs. People mention a heaviness and that the negative energy is palpable at times. Some people comment that they don't know why, but they don't like it down there. One visitor claimed that his chest started pounding for no reason, and he said that "he just had to get out of there." Low, inaudible moans have been heard, and one staff member claimed to have once heard, "Go away."

Famed psychic Greta Alexander once toured Susan's old home. Once she was finished reading the house, she commented that the home was indeed home to several different spirits, namely Susan, her cousin Flora and Susan's mother and father. But there is also a dark entity in the house that refuses to leave; it wants the house for itself. Greta believed that during one of Susan's numerous séances, she unintentionally invoked this entity and invited it into the house. She believed that Susan had trouble with this strong entity ever since. Greta also believed that Susan's, Flora's and her parents' spiritual energy all combined to be stronger than this entity and that, in death, they remain in the house to keep this negative entity suppressed and confined to the basement. Greta finished up by saying that, entity or not, the Lawrences would still likely be haunting the home in a positive manner due to the family bond they all shared and the affection they had for the fantastic home that Susan built.

The home is still alive today with spirits.

# THE INN AT 835 AND BELL

Born in 1870, Bell Miller was one of Springfield's first professional businesswomen, starting her own floral business in her early twenties. Her florist shop catered to the wealthy residents of the Aristocracy Hill neighborhood of Springfield, and she became quite successful. Bell Miller's greenhouse once encompassed nearly an entire city block. By the turn of the century, Bell had become wealthy.

In 1909, she had Springfield's first modern apartment building constructed on the corner of 2nd and Canedy Streets. It was designed by the known architectural firm of Helme and Helme. The building contained six luxury apartments, including one for herself. The building was completed with several open balconies on each floor and large ornate fireplaces throughout, and the oak trim work was milled with impressive architectural detail. The building is in the National Register of Historic Places. To this day, it retains most of its original architectural details and historic charm inside and out.

In 1994, a local businessman purchased the building, and each of the apartments was converted into luxury guestrooms. It is now called the Inn at 835, Springfield's finest bed-and-breakfast accommodations. Each guestroom maintains the old historic charm, with luxurious accommodations such as private baths and Jacuzzis, and some have original working fireplaces and access to open balconies.

Legend has it that Bell Miller has never left her old home. She had a first-floor apartment on the south side, now a dining and reception area. Much of the haunted activity here seems to have resulted not from some tragic or untimely death, but perhaps out of a love for or a bond with her place. Bell Miller's life accomplishments were astounding for a woman in her time, and her beautiful apartment building was the culmination of her success. Perhaps this is the reason she remains in her old building today.

Bell was not only known for her charitable nature and kindness within the community, but she was also kind and sociable with her tenants and their guests. She is said to have greeted her tenants in the front entryway coming home from their workday, and guests of her tenants to the apartment building, with candy from a crystal candy dish once kept on a reception desk. Bell also socialized in a front parlor as well, and she just might still be greeting guests and socializing today. There have been numerous bizarre occurrences here, witnessed by guests and employees alike over many years.

Some believe that Bell still greets guests checking in at the front desk with a faint garbled voice that says, "Hello there" or "Welcome home." Guests hearing the faint voice will turn to respond, but no one else is seen standing there. The inn has the original crystal candy dish once owned by Bell that she used to greet tenants and visitors. And today, guests have also been distracted by the unmistakable faint sound of glass-on-glass *tink*. They turn to look in the direction of the sound, but nothing or no one is seen. Bell has been gone since the 1940s, but today the sounds of a crystal lid being replaced on a candy dish can sometimes still be heard even though the lid to the original crystal candy dish has long been removed.

Bell's apparition has also been seen by guests describing a womanly figure darting across the hall or through a doorway in various areas of the inn as well. Witnesses describe her with hair pulled back, wearing a long-sleeved blouse and a full-length skirt in a style unlike any fashion today. Many people seem to see her out of the corner of their eyes for just a split second, but others claim to have seen her briskly pass by the front desk while they were coming in the front door of the inn. It's interesting that front entry area witnesses all claim that her movement was from right to left, as if she might be walking into her apartment once located right there. The only picture of Bell Miller also hangs on the wall in front entry area today right next to her former apartment door.

Some people also believe that they feel Bell's presence or feel like someone is watching them in the breakfast room. One couple eating breakfast claimed that the more they talked about Bell's ghost, the stronger they could feel her presence with them, adding that it felt like she was standing right there next to them, but of course no one was seen. Others speak of similar sensations in

*Above*: This is an original photograph taken during a haunted tour. Some believe that they can see the ghostly apparition of Bell Mill standing on the landing inside the front door, where she once greeted visitors to the home. *Garret Moffett.*

*Left*: The only known photograph of Bell Miller. *Conn's Hospitality.*

the front parlor area where she was also known to socialize. People relaxing in the wingback chairs sometimes sense that someone is watching them. Others claim to feel a woman's presence when a sudden inexplicable breeze flutters by. An innkeeper was occasionally annoyed by a particular book in the front parlor that seemed to repeatedly find its way onto the floor despite re-shelving the book herself numerous times. She said it was like someone was seeking attention or playing a prank. Placing the book elsewhere or calling out "Enough!" seemed to quell the attention-getting behavior until the next time.

Innkeepers occasionally deal with little pranks and nuisances that are mostly annoying. But there is one prank that is attributed to Bell that certainly got the attention of one of the innkeepers. One slow fall night, the front desk received a call from one of the rooms upstairs. The woman's voice sounded concerned; she said she couldn't get the thermostat to work, and her room was cold. The innkeeper told the woman that she'd be right up. But as she began to ascend the stairs, she suddenly stopped and recalled that that particular room was to be empty that night. She went back and checked the registry; the room was, in fact, vacant. But the innkeeper was sure that the call came from that room, so she went straight up to the room. She found the door closed and locked. It was inn policy to keep vacant room doors open. Concerned and equally perplexed, she knocked on the door, but no one answered. Using her passkey, the innkeeper entered the room and found the room dark and empty. But she was suddenly taken aback by the sharp coldness in the room; it was so cold that she could see her own breath in the air. Now aware of a presence in the room, she cautiously backed out of the room, locking the door behind her, and considered the room occupied for the night.

Then there's the strange prankster activity with the elevator. Guests and innkeepers repeatedly claim that regardless of which button they press, the elevator occasionally stops on a different floor. Sometimes the innkeepers will have to call out, "Enough, take me to the third floor!" They've even been known to give up on the elevator and take the stairs. The elevator doors have also been known to open by themselves when someone approaches the call button, just like at Springfield High School. Repeated maintenance and inspections on the elevator never reveal anything wrong.

But one of the more bizarre encounters involved a couple at the front desk speaking with the innkeeper and writing down some information on a small notepad. All of a sudden, the notepad inexplicably went flying out of the woman's hand and landed on the floor several feet away. Perplexed, the three just looked at one another and shrugged it off. The woman picked up the notepad from the floor and continued to write, and then *swoosh*! The notepad went flying out of her hand again, as if someone just threw it away. The innkeeper teasingly said, "We must have a ghost" and shrugged it off, not wanting to draw any more attention.

Guests have reported strange activity during their stay at the inn. They sometimes share their stories in journals or notes left behind in rooms for the next guest or the innkeeper. Stories from guests suggest that they are more intrigued than frightened by their unexplained encounters. One couple who happen to be staying in the "cold" room on their anniversary had an unusual night. Late that night, while his wife was sleeping, the man was sitting in a wingback chair across the room reading a book by the fireplace. Thinking it was odd that a cold chill overcame the room while by the fireplace, he looked up and saw a very faint shadowy figure standing in the bathroom doorway next to the bed where his wife was sleeping. In a second, it vanished right before his eyes. It happened in such a fleeting moment that he wasn't sure it had happened and didn't give it much though, at least at first.

Just several minutes later, the man, still reading in his chair, heard his sleeping wife say, "Quit it." He ignored her, but moments later, she again muttered, "Quit it." This time, the man responded, and she told him to quit messing with her feet. He told her it wasn't him, as he was across the room in the chair. She sat right up in bed and claimed that someone was tickling her feet. Neither claimed to be frightened by the night's events; they said if it was a ghost, it was just playing around. He mentioned that he thought he saw someone standing in the doorway to the bathroom just moments ago, and his wife responded with a smile and shifted herself to the opposite side of the bed away from the bathroom door.

Another couple staying in a different room spoke about sleeping one night when the man suddenly woke to the sound of people talking in the room. Within a moment, the voices stopped, and the man thought maybe it had just been part of a dream. He went back to sleep. The next morning, the couple was getting dressed and ready for the day when the woman asked the man who he was talking to last night. Apparently, she heard the talking as well and had thought her husband was talking in his sleep.

For all of the bizarre and ghostly activity at the inn, the antics are benign and harmless. Bell is still around, looking after her building, and she seems to enjoy the company of the guests at the charming old inn. But there seems to be a mysterious spirit that haunts lower entryway of the inn, and he may not be so nice. A tall, dark, shadowy man has made his ghostly appearance on a handful of occasions and has been caught on camera in the front door entry area. The mysterious and elusive shadow man has only been seen a few times, and he's only been encountered in the front entry area, nowhere else in the inn. When seen, he appears to be standing in a sort of arrogant pose and gives off a vibe of trespassing, as though he doesn't want people in his space.

Innkeepers working around the front desk have, on a few occasions, looked down at the front door to see the shadow man standing there seemingly looking right back at the innkeeper, who's overcome with an uncomfortable sense of foreboding. One innkeeper working late at night left the inn for her car in the parking lot when she got the notion to turn around, only to see the shadow man standing on the sidewalk right in front of the inn at the door. As you can imagine, she briskly walked to her car and felt relieved to be off work for the night. She did not turn around for a second look. The man's identity is not known for certain, but a former maintenance and door man who worked for Bell was murdered at his home several blocks away. His murder remains unsolved today.

Today, the Inn at 835 continues to function as the finest B&B accommodation and banquet facilities in Springfield. Bell Miller is a part of the inn, and she will no doubt continue to add to the luxurious mystique and charm of the old inn.

# THE SPLIT-HOUSE PHANTOM

It was 1935, and the Great Depression was not yet over in Springfield. Gertrude and Raymond Meyers were newlyweds in their twenties when they moved into their modest home late that summer. Their house looked similar to other nearby houses, but it looked exactly like the house right next door. The newlyweds were just grateful to have a roof over their heads in such hard times.

Gertrude was a high school teacher with ambition to be a writer someday. Raymond worked as a printer at night, and he was gone most evenings and nights. They didn't have much time together, as one was coming home from work while the other was leaving for work. Gertrude had to spend her evenings home alone until 3:30 a.m., when Raymond came home, and this made for some lonely nights.

With fall settling in and the air getting cooler, it was time to close up the windows in preparation for the coming winter. Gertrude was feeling down since she wasn't able to have the windows open, allowing in a breeze and the outside noises to keep her company on those lonely evenings. With the house closed up, Gertrude became more aware of her surroundings. Something was different about the house, and it made her uncomfortable. Gertrude sensed that there was a presence. She was not as alone as she had previously thought, and this unwelcome presence was not good company.

Night after night, Gertrude closed her bedroom door and climbed into a cold and empty bed. Soon the phantom walker began his nightly torment. At 10:30 p.m. almost every night, she heard heavy footsteps start at the front door, walk across the hall, methodically climb the stairs right to her bedroom door and suddenly stop. She would wake from her sleep, hide under her covers and painstakingly listen to the phantom footsteps. By the time they reached her bedroom door, she was paralyzed with fear. She sensed that it was a man because the footsteps were so heavy. The phantom walker didn't show up every night, much to her relief, but when he did, it was always at 10:30 p.m. sharp. Nevertheless, Gertrude began to wake every night at that time in anticipation of the phantom walker, and she began to lose sleep.

Gertrude was reluctant to tell her husband anything. She didn't want him to think that she was being ridiculous or making it up because she was lonely at night. But the stalker was unnerving her, and it was getting too much to bear. She had to do something. Gertrude decided to summon her strength and courage to confront the phantom walker the next time he reached her bedroom door. Just as expected, at 10:30 p.m. sharp the footsteps began. She heard every footstep coming closer to her door, and then the footsteps stopped right at the threshold of her door. With all of her might, she yanked open the door, only to find no one standing there. She looked down the hall, but it was empty. For the next week, every time she heard the footsteps stop, she opened the door hoping to see who her phantom stalker was. No one was ever there.

While Gertrude was dealing with this, Raymond was having his own inexplicable experiences with the phantom footsteps. He got home from work about 3:30 a.m., and he would first go down into the basement and stoke up the coal furnace before going to bed. While down in the basement, he would hear footsteps walking across the floor above him and wonder why his wife was up so late. But he would find her moments later fast asleep in their bed. Raymond, sleeping late, also heard the phantom footsteps in the morning outside their bedroom door after his wife had left for work.

Raymond decided to ask his wife if she ever got up in the night and came downstairs while he was stoking the furnace down in the basement. He told her about the footsteps, and she was relieved to be able to finally tell him about the phantom walker that tortured her almost every night. Their stories were similar—always hearing footsteps but never seeing anyone. They were both curious who the phantom walker was and why he was here.

Winter came and went, and the phantom walker persisted. Gertrude and Raymond gradually became used to the footsteps and weren't so unnerved by their phantom walker as much anymore, but they still wondered who he was and why he was there. A possible answer would soon come to them.

Spring arrived, and Gertrude was happy to have the windows open again with the sun shining in and warming the house. She decided to plant a garden to occupy her time after school. One afternoon while she was working in the garden, she was talking with her next-door neighbors, who were also working in their garden. A grandmother and grandson lived in the identical house next door. They got to talking about their houses and how they were identical. Gertrude mentioned the phantom walker that had belabored them since they moved in late the previous summer. The neighbors were amazed to hear about the footsteps because they, too, had been experiencing the same phantom footsteps in their own house for some time now. The phantom walker followed the same routine in both houses. At 10:30 p.m., the footsteps began at the front door and then moved across the hall and up the stairs before stopping at the master bedroom door. Just like in the Meyers house, they didn't hear the footsteps every night, and when they did, no one was ever seen. The neighbor told them that their houses were joined together at one time, making it a duplex. The owner living in one of the duplexes committed suicide at one point in the house. The new property owner decided to split the duplex apart, making it two separate but identical houses.

They all decided that the phantom night walker was probably the former homeowner who died by his own hand. With his former house now split into two separate houses, perhaps his wandering spirit was confused, and with both houses familiar to him, in death he alternated haunting each house on different nights.

Over time, the phantom walker's heavy footsteps faded into silence. The phantom walker is heard no more.

# GHOSTLY EDWARDS PLACE

Edwards Place was originally built in 1833 for Dr. Thomas Houghan, but he sold the story-and-a-half home and fifteen acres of land to Benjamin and Helen Edwards in 1843. The Edwards family renovated the home, adding fifteen rooms to create its present-day appearance. The beautiful Italianate-style mansion is well preserved today. It's the oldest house on its original foundation, and some will argue that it's the oldest house in Springfield.

Benjamin Edwards, a lawyer, was part of a prominent social and political family in Springfield and had plenty of wealth and social and political power. His father, Ninian Edwards Sr., was the first territorial governor of Illinois and later a senator and third governor of Illinois. Benjamin's brother Albert was the founder of AG Edwards, an investment firm still in business today. His other brother, Ninian W. Edwards Jr., was a state politician who married Elizabeth Todd, the oldest sister of Mary Todd Lincoln.

The famous "courting couch" from Elizabeth's home where the Lincolns were first introduced and subsequently courted is now on display at Edwards Place, Benjamin and Helen's home. Mary Lincoln and Helen Edwards were good friends and shared that bond for life.

Edwards Place was one of several Springfield homes that were host to Springfield's social elite events and dinner parties. Edwards Place was also host to scores of picnics on the grounds during the summers. Entertaining was a matter of high society back then. The men might be sitting in one of the parlors of the home smoking cigars and discussing the latest politics, while the ladies might be in a different parlor engaged in the latest courtship gossip. However, it would have been no surprise to find Mary Lincoln in the parlor with the men debating politics. The Edwardses and the Lincolns ran in the same circles and were guests in each other's homes. The two men were both lawyers and had faced each other in the courtroom more than one hundred times, and they even worked as co-counsel at times. Although both men were Whigs, they did not agree on matters or politics at times. And when the Whig Party split, Lincoln became a Republican and Edwards a Democrat. Ben Edwards supported Douglas and held political rallies for him at Edwards Place during the 1858 senatorial campaign.

To learn what it would have been like to socialize with the Lincolns, you only need to walk through the front door of Edwards Place, now owned by the Springfield Art Association. The historical interpretation of Edwards Place today tells the story of Benjamin and Helen Edwards, their connection to the Lincoln family and their lavish social lifestyle from 1843 to 1909. The home is an open-air museum where you can walk through the entire house among an amazing collections of nineteenth-century antique furnishings. The old mansion has a sensational history, and within the walls of Edwards Place are old ghosts from a time long past.

Edwards Place does an annual Haunted Nights of History where the site interpreters dress up as Edwards family members and tell stories about the family and the home to visitors while stationed throughout the home. But the ghosts in Edwards Place find ways to make their own presence known and, in some cases, tell their own stories.

The strange and ghostly encounters at Edwards Place are thought to be the result of several different entities haunting the old mansion. Tom and Alice, grandchildren of Ben and Helen, are thought to haunt the home, reliving their playful youth. The spirit of a former home servant may also linger. Perhaps there are others.

During one of the Haunted Nights of History, there were several visitors who suddenly felt ill when they reached the top of the stairs, and they had to immediately retreat outside for fresh air. They claimed that they could feel a presence, and at the same time, interpreters standing in the bedroom to the right of the stairs also claimed that they felt a presence as the ladies were bustling down the stairs they just came up. Voice recordings in this area revealed a young girl's voice that clearly said her name was "Alice," and in recordings, she expresses her dissatisfaction about the bed covers on her bed, which is amazing because at the time staff members didn't like the particular bed covering either! People have not only sensed her little girl spirit, but some

The first-floor parlor of Edwards Place, perhaps haunted by the grandchildren of Benjamin and Helen Edwards. *Garret Moffett.*

also claim to have felt a little tug on their shirt or coat while in the bedroom. Once a visitor to the home reported seeing a ghostly apparition of a woman in that same bedroom looking out the window. The witness thought at first that the woman was a costumed interpreter in period clothing, but when the woman disappeared from her sight a moment later, she realized that she had just seen someone from days long past.

The playful spirit of Tom is one of the most interactive spirits encountered. Tom likes to hang out in the back parlor of the home, which is filled with antique children's toys. What ghost boy wouldn't want to hang out in the most fun room in the house? If there was any doubt as to the existence of young Tom, it was laid to rest when a voice recording was made in the playroom capturing a young boy's ghostly voice answering direct questions. One evening, there were eight people sitting in a circle on the floor with a recorder in the center. When someone asked if Tom was present—the response was clear: "Tom has come to play."

Although the grandchildren of Ben and Helen did not die in the house, their presence in the house has been encountered and recorded.

The playroom, full of nineteenth-century children's toys. A voice recording in this room captured a young boy's voice saying, "Tom has come to play." *Garret Moffett.*

Both children lived through adulthood, so why might they be haunting Edwards Place as children? Is this even possible? For many kids, childhood was a magical time, especially for kids who were surrounded by loving parents and doting grandparents known for spoiling grandkids. Childhood was an innocent time not yet tainted by the troubles of the world. And Edwards Place was a lively home with lots of excitement and events going on, especially the picnics with homemade ice cream. Perhaps in death, Alice and Tom return to their childhoods at Grandma's, perhaps the best of times in their lives. But if there are ghostly children playing around Edwards Place, they would certainly need supervision. There's also the spirit of an indentured servant who once worked and lived in the home and no doubt would have tended to the grandchildren.

Ghosts seem to like to play with alarms, and it's no surprise that staff management have been called to the house at night to reset a tripped alarm. Here, the alarm is usually tripped in the kitchen and dining areas, where the family and servants would have spent considerable time. As many times as the alarm has tripped, no one has been found in the home, and there's no sign of attempted entry; the alarm sensors are always in good working order.

Visitors in the dining area have reported time and time again about a feeling a presence and experiencing sudden cold spots that gave them a chill as if someone just walked behind them. One visitor claimed that while experiencing a cold spot, she also witnessed a wisp of white light streak across a doorway and was gone. Voice recordings in the area have revealed a woman's soft, unintelligible voice, and to some people it sounds like the voice of someone who has some sort of accent. Perhaps this is the same spirit encountered in the attic area where the servants' bedroom likely was located and remnants of an old servant call system can still be seen.

Staff members working in the attic area have talked about seeing shadows moving about but can't explain where the shadow is coming from. Little bottle cap–sized spots of light called "sprites" can be seen zipping through the air in random patterns that abruptly change directions before zipping away and disappearing from sight. And others just don't like it up there but will claim to feel like they're invading the space of an unseen presence. The same dark shadow has been seen coming down the servants' back stairs from the attic but disappears from sight during the descent, unnerving unsuspecting witnesses.

The Edwards family did host an indentured servant for one year in the house. After that year, for whatever reasons, the family employed Irish housekeeping staff. A life or job of servitude is certainly not glamorous, but for whichever servant is still haunting the house today, perhaps they had formed a bond with the grandchildren and remain in the house looking after them today.

# THE HICKOX HOUSE SPIRITS

Virgil Hickox was born in 1806, just three years before Abraham Lincoln, and by 1834 he had moved to Springfield from Jefferson County, New York. In 1839, Hickox married Marie Catherine Cabanis and built a home on Capitol Avenue between 5th and 6th Streets. Hickox fathered ten children, but only six survived. Today, the Hickox House is the oldest residential structure in immediate downtown Springfield. Although the home has undergone several renovations over the years, the home retains much of its original architectural features such as several fireplaces and detailed woodwork. The home retains an amazing amount of Springfield history and is host to incredible haunted history and paranormal activity. Scores of people have experienced the haunted history of the Hickox House, and this home has made believers out of nonbelievers' time and time again. The paranormal activity here can be downright frightful and even violent on occasion.

Hickox had only an elementary education, but he became an entrepreneur of all sorts, investing in his own mercantile store and becoming president of Springfield's Savings Bank and founder of the Chicago-Alton Railroad. He also cofounded the town of Lincoln, Illinois. Hickox was an important political figure, acting as chairman of the Democratic State Committee, but the only political office he held was canal commissioner of the Chicago and Michigan Canal, the largest nineteenth-century canal in the United States at the time. Hickox was a Democrat and a good friend of Stephen Douglas, who visited the Hickox home on occasion. It's believed that Lincoln was received here as well. Hickox worked as Douglas's campaign manager in the 1858 senatorial bid against Abraham Lincoln and said that his greatest life accomplishment was Douglas's success. Nevertheless, Hickox and Lincoln were cordial to each other like gentlemen despite opposing views. Virgil Hickox held the last letter dictated by Stephen Douglas, dated May 10, 1861, in which Douglas declared that there would be only two political parties, one of patriots and the other of traitors.

After the death of Hickox in February 1880, his stately Capitol Avenue home began its long connection to Springfield's cultural fabric. In 1890, the home became the first site for the Sangamo Club, a sort of private club for men. After World War I, the club moved into a different location, and the Sangamon County coroner, who lived upstairs and ran his funeral business downstairs, became the new tenant. The basement is where the embalming procedures took place. The basement window, known as a coffin window, remains today on the west side; it's where coffins and bodies were slid inside on a ramp. During Prohibition, the basement was used as a speakeasy where people could drink in secrecy. A secret call button that would alert patrons to an impending raid also still exists in the basement. However, when Prohibition was over, the basement became a legal liquor establishment. A popular local restaurant and tavern called Norb Andy's Tabarin opened its doors and for the next fifty years became a favorite watering hole for locals and politicians from just down the street at the capitol. (A tabarin is a name for a local place of small plates, drinks and entertainment.) Imagine the tales this house could tell—the heated politics of Lincoln's day, the fellowship of a private men's club, the preservation and mourning of the dead, the drunken merriment of the old speakeasy and the good times and bonds made between friends at Norb Andy's Tabarin. A lot of emotions have been imprinted on the environment of this old historic house.

The haunted activity in this home is incredible, and you might think that it results from the old mortuary once here. But the home seems to be haunted by a variety of spirits, some of which may not necessarily be connected to the house. This may suggest that the home may contain a portal of sorts, an open window between two planes of existence that enables spirits to stream back and forth.

The Hickox House has been widely investigated for several years by a number of paranormal groups yielding a great deal of ghostly evidence. The first paranormal team in this house was this author, team members and clergy in 2007. It didn't take long to realize that investigating this place was not for the faint of heart or the amateur ghost hunter. Spirits here can be both benign and malevolent.

Audible sounds that may or may not be attributed to an old house settling can be heard, such as whispering, tapping, knocking, footsteps, breathing and sounds of doors opening or closing. Digital recordings reveal voices, and when those voices respond to direct questions asked, it's pretty convincing evidence that spirits are present. Recorded responses such as "yes," "no," "where's mommy," "talking to you," "not here," "where is it," "the ball," "go away" and "I'm looking" have all been heard. But some responses can be quite chilling, like "I'm dead." One very unsettling guttural voice was heard on a recording proclaiming, "Not dead." Breathing, wind, growls and other bizarre sounds have all been recorded.

"Sprites" can be seen in the home with the naked eye. These are little dots of bright light that zing briskly through the air, abruptly changing directions of flight. Orbs of light can also be seen in the house with the naked eye, which are larger balls of softer light, and they can be transparent or translucent and even take on different colors. These orbs are more frequently captured in photos, but they've also been seen frequently in the house taking flight right in front of people. Orbs can frequently be explained as dust particles or matter in the air reflecting off the camera flash or camera artifacts like light reflecting off the lens of the camera.

The Virgil Hickox House just after the turn on the century. *Sangamon Valley Collection.*

This photo, taken on Memorial Day 1887, shows Civil War soldiers standing in front of the Hickox House. *Sangamon Valley Collection.*

While setting up for an investigation one night in the house, an orb about eight inches in diameter came right into the room, and six people (scampering to get a camera turned on) could clearly see this curious-acting orb. It did a half-circle loop and wisped out of the room. The event lasted only three to four seconds. It was an unusual but amazing encounter to say the least.

The same night, a photo taken revealed a blue arc of light against a black background. Blue arcs are thought to indicate the presence of very strong and sometimes malevolent energy. It is a message to proceed with great caution or, better, to back away.

On several occasions, ectoplasmic bursts have been witnessed. This looks like a fog-like mist or smoke wafting through the air without any plausible explanation for the cause. But when this mist seems to be dimensional and take shape of a young child walking, these encounters will intrigue the most seasoned ghost hunters and frighten the faint of heart.

There seem to be several spirits in the house, and through voice recordings, it's been determined that some of them don't seem to have any connection to the house. Aside from a portal in the house, why else might they be here? Some sensitive people suggest that spirits could have been brought here or attracted to the house because of the other spirits in the house.

When the old funeral home opened in the house, Springfield was still recovering from the infamous flu epidemic of 1918 that killed nearly four hundred citizens. Springfield was under quarantine, and temporary hospitals were set up around town to take on the overflow of patients. The death rate continued, and funeral homes were busy for months, including the funeral home inside the Hickox House. Although the epidemic hit all ages, it was children who were hardest hit by the killer flu. It's been suggested that these spirits are lost and seeking similar spirits or even loved ones.

One such spirit caught on numerous recordings represents herself as twelve-year-old Alice, who seems to be in a perpetual search for her mother. Other recordings capture the voice of Alice calling out, "Mommy." With so many recordings of Alice looking for her mother, it seemed so sad that this little spirit girl was unable to fully cross over. There were several attempts, with the help of clergy, to either help her find her mother or fully cross her over to the other side, but all attempts have failed. She remains in the house. When recording and asking Alice about other spirits in the house, the voice simply states "Afraid" with the tone of a stressed child.

It's believed that Alice is referring to the "shadow man," which seems to be a dominant and malevolent spirit in the house. The child spirits in the house seem to be frightened of him, and at times so are the living. The shadow man is arrogant and does not like intruders in his space. This seems to be a common denominator with shadow spirits. This spirit is believed to have choked and slapped people entering into the house on more than one occasion. One such night on a tour through the house, a Springfield firefighter was slapped in the face by an unseen hand. The man was standing in a room listening to the tour guide when he suddenly felt a stinging to his face. When he commented that his face was stinging, a light was shined on his face and revealed a bright red fresh handprint on his cheek. The handprint was obvious, and no one heard the slap nor saw anything. Astonished, the fireman said, "I felt the sting. It hurt." An unnerved fireman is an uncommon thing, but this fireman chose to step outside and get some fresh air. He later commented, still in disbelief, "I just came along for the stories. I didn't really think anything like ghosts were real. I don't see how this is possible."

The fireman isn't the only one who's been "touched" in the house. A tour guide one night was prepping people before going into the house, giving instructions that if anyone began to feel ill or received a push to step outside for a few minutes. A man with his wife commented that the guide was really "hyping it up." The group went in, and within five minutes the wife was bolting out of the house in a full panic onto the front porch, with her husband close behind. The guide checking on her found her quite upset and crying. The guide was told to look at the back of her neck, and sure enough, there was fresh blood oozing from very distinct fingernail scratches across the back of her neck. The husband was angry and confused as to how this could have happened. He said, "I was standing right there with her. There was no way anyone stepped up to her and did that without me seeing it." The wife required some minor first aid and refused to go back into the house, understandably. The couple came back the next weekend for another tour of the house, but when it came time for entry, she refused to go back in. The husband went in and explored without any major incident, but he claimed that he sensed something was there not of this world. Other people touring through the house have also made claims of being pushed or nudged in the back, as if someone were trying to move them along, especially down the stairs.

Not much is known about the shadow man, who attempts to remain elusive. But evidence pieced together from voice recordings and psychic mediums suggests that he may have been a mechanic or engineer of some kind and likely known to be a man of poor temperamental disposition in life

Virgil Hickox.
*Sangamon Valley
Collection.*

and also in death. It's also been suggested that his body had passed through the funeral home at one time. It's believed that it is his malevolent spirit that chases and torments the child spirits in the house.

As for any members of the Hickox family haunting the house, there has been some contact made with Marie and Mary Hickox, Virgil's wife and daughter. But evidence also yields that a variety of spirits can be found in the house, which leads some to believe that there's a portal in the house, a window to the other side where spirits can come and go between realms. Repeated attempts to close the portal and free the house of so many spirits have always failed. But with the assistance of clergy, it is now believed that St. Peter stands guard and watches over the portal, helping lost spirits find their way into the light. Unfortunately, and for whatever reason, other spirits remain lost, unable to cross over or find the light of God.

However, the basement of the house, where the body preparations were made for the funeral home above, has another kind of haunted activity entirely. In 1937, a salty man named Norbert Anderson opened up Norb Andy's Tabarin. He was never in the U.S. Navy, but he liked the fisherman décor of taverns back east and he fancied the same décor for his tabarin.

The Hickox House and Norb Andy's in modern day. *Garret Moffett.*

The décor of knotted pine, fishnets, buoys and whale oil lamps, along with Norb's warm hospitality, gave Norb Andy's something few places have: tradition.

It was Norb's personality and character that gave his establishment life. Patrons here knew one another well, and Norb knew his patrons by name. He warmly greeted customers when they came in and thanked them when they left, and in no time, he had a strong and faithful clientele. Employees and customers became loyal friends, and it was the best of times: good food, good drinks, good music and good friends. In no time, Norb's became a favorite place for the politicians from the statehouse just down the street. Customers could be sitting in a seat where well-known politicians such as Henry Horner, Jim Thompson, Adlai Stevenson or Alan Dixon once sat in one of their many visits. In fact, Norb's had a small room in the back that became known as the "Scuttlebutt" room. Here, politicians would hold unofficial and casual meetings with other politicians and lobbyists. Some people suggest that more deals and legislation were created and passed in this back room than at the statehouse down the street.

Norb was protective of his customer base too. If you asked him what his customers drank, he would tell you that they don't drink—they come in for the food. Norb's had become a Springfield institution. It was the place to go. Norb loved his place, and he ran it for more than forty years. When Norb finally passed away, it was the end of an era for this neighborhood bar. Last call had passed, and the party was over for Norb…or was it?

Norb's was reopened with new owners sometime after 2005, and the party was back on. People were delighted that the old neighborhood bar opened again, and they returned for another stretch of good drinks, food, music and, of course, good friends. The new Norb's kept the name and the original décor and the charm. It's believed that Norb himself returned to the party as well, pulling pranks on employees and customers, perhaps to let folks know that he's still around looking after his old tabarin.

Numerous inexplicable things can happen here, from downright strange to heart-jumping. Granted, alcohol is often involved, but stories are also told by the sober. Apparently, Norb can be quite a prankster.

Patrons engaged in conversation with friends will reach for their drink, only to find that their glass has been moved or even switched with other drinks on the table without anyone noticing. Friends pranking friends you might think of course, but what about when the drink glass slides across the bar or table a few inches, astonishing witnesses. Bartenders have claimed to set a drink down on the waitress station mat, but when the waitress goes to retrieve the drink, it's missing, and no one had been seen near the waitress station. Bartenders have bottles arranged a certain way in the racks so they can just reach for bottles without having to read them. At times they would find bottles completely rearranged out of order without anyone else behind the bar. And bartenders and waitresses aren't typically the kind of people who easily fall for bar pranks, especially repeatedly, and they don't usually appreciate a customer who repeatedly pulls inconveniencing bar pranks either. We all know there are rules in a bar!

One of the more frightful pranks pulled by Norb involves people utilizing the restrooms. Patrons will joke with other patrons to not look in the mirror in the bathroom or you might meet ol' Norb himself. At times, patrons have indeed regretted looking into the mirror, and for a heart-thumping split second, a flash of a man smiling is seen standing behind them in the mirror. Patrons quickly turn around to see no one standing there. It's been known to happen in either restroom when someone comes running out of the bathroom in a huff. Norb's ghostly apparition is unique. He was known to wear a polyester blue leisure suit or type of sports coat popular in the '70s. People will say that the man looks real enough, but at certain angles, his clothing gives off a bluish color. This bluish apparition of Norb seems to be seen passing by the Scuttlebutt room or walking up the stairs out the door at the end of the night. Some employees are amused and comfortable enough to call out, "Good night, Norb!" He's also been seen in a fraction of a second sitting on a corner barstool that he frequently occupied.

One afternoon, a new and young bartender was opening for the day and had a frightful encounter with a pranking Norb. She had only been opened for a few minutes and hadn't heard anyone come in, but she turned around and was startled by an older man sitting at the bar on the corner barstool. He was wearing a blue jacket that was well out of fashion, she thought. She needed to retrieve a bottle from storage to stock the bar and told the man that she'd be right back. He didn't say a word. When she came back a moment later, the man was gone. She thought that was weird, as she didn't hear him leave and he didn't even order a drink. As she looked at the spot where the man had been sitting, her eyes fell on a picture on the wall behind the barstool. It was the same man, and she was overcome with goosebumps. She realized that she had just seen old Norb himself, and he had passed away some years prior. She even commented that she could smell his aftershave. Other patrons finally came in, much to her relief.

Another encounter involved several people sitting at the bar, with the bartender working away. A man standing at the corner of the bar where old Norb's barstool sat had noticed Norb's picture on the wall and asked about it. A few patrons started telling some stories about Norb's ghostly pranks. Moments later, the man, who was mildly amused by the stories, was pranked by Norb when a stack of menus sitting on the bar suddenly flew off the bar, sailed through the air across the room and fell to the floor. Everyone at the bar was astonished, and the bartender was visibly shaken. No one had touched the menus, and they weren't precariously stacked and simply fell on the floor—they flew through the air across the room, according to several witnesses.

At the end of Norb's life, perhaps he just couldn't give up his bar and all the good times he had and the friends he made through the years. Norbert Anderson may still be haunting and watching over his old establishment, no doubt because of a bond and love for it, as well as the memories. For Norb, the good times continue.

A word to the wise for anyone going to look for an encounter with Alice in the upper part of the house: tread lightly. In fact, this is a spirit to stay away from altogether. Evidence suggests that Alice is not the spirit of a twelve-year-old girl who may have died in the flu epidemic. Alice is most likely a nonhuman entity that represents itself as a young little girl searching for her mommy in an effort to find and trick a human host to occupy and take form. Anyone feeling sorry for little Alice and openly expressing any type of sorrow for her is opening themselves up for an attachment. This attachment has occurred before, and this entity is extremely difficult to get rid of once the attachment happens.

# SPRINGFIELD HIGH SCHOOL AND A DISTURBED CEMETERY

The ghostly stories here begin with a custodian checking for a water leak in the basement of the school. Suddenly, in the dim light, he saw a young girl about ten years of age wearing a floral dress standing among a group of pipes and looking at him. Startled, he nonetheless thought that a student was just goofing off, with her strange appearance and menacing look. He rebuked her presence: "What are you doing down here? You're not supposed to be down here!" And without a sound, she vanished into thin air right before his eyes.

Springfield High School is built directly on the site of the former Hutchinson Cemetery of the 1850s. John Hutchinson was a cabinet maker and undertaker. In 1843, he started a small family cemetery on a plot of land that he owned. There was a city cemetery a few blocks away, but it was small and inadequate for the needs of the city. Before long, the Hutchinson Cemetery had become the preferred burial ground for the city, eventually encompassing six acres of land and about seven hundred burials. The most notable burial in the cemetery was Eddie Lincoln, the second son of the Lincolns, who died in 1850 just three months shy of his fourth birthday. Among the seven hundred graves of Springfield's early pioneers were quite a number of child burials. Even the historical marker in front of the high school mentions the high number of child burials within the old cemetery.

In the mid-1800s, the capitol city was still a rough prairie town, and life without many conveniences was hard, harsh and unfair. Accidents were commonplace. Cemetery records tell of a child who was scalded to death, another killed by a lightning strike, another killed by falling brick from a construction site and another killed by a runaway carriage. The list goes on.

Disease was also commonplace, and illnesses were difficult to treat and control back then without modern medicine such as antibiotics. Springfield was hit hard by diseases such as measles and typhoid fever. The bringer of death had no prejudices, and children were often the hardest hit. A fever raging through a community would instill fear, and everyone was in danger, as there was little knowledge of just how to stop the epidemic. It wasn't uncommon for cemeteries to receive multiple or mass burials in a single day when a fever besieged a community. In some cases, the dead would be wrapped up in the very sheets they died in and buried at night so the public would not attend the funerals. Clothes, possessions and sometimes the home would be burned to stop the spread of disease. Great numbers of pioneer families had gaps in their family trees from losing one or more family members, just like how the Lincoln family lost three of their four boys to illness and disease.

However, in 1876, a new city ordinance prevented any further burials within the new city limits. Rather than simply close the cemetery, it was decided to remove the entire cemetery from city limits. Thus began the removal of six hundred corpses to their new place of burial. Bodies were reinterred in different cemeteries, but the majority of the bodies were buried at Oak Ridge Cemetery north of town. However, some of the town folk who had decided to gather and watch the disinterment claimed that the number of corpses removed didn't match the number of recorded burials, believing that at least one hundred bodies remained behind. Why would bodies be left behind? It's quite possible that some of the graves of the poor, unknown or indigent were not moved. Graves get lost due to poor recordkeeping or lost to time and Mother Nature. Any grave markers made from wood wouldn't last, and some graves may not have been marked at all. Any bodies buried in pine coffins would decay rapidly, leaving little left to move. But there could also be a more sinister reason bodies were left behind. Whomever was paying the disinterment bill could have been trying to save some money by leaving one hundred or so bodies behind.

With the bodies moved to Oak Ridge Cemetery, the Hutchinson land remained empty. Investors and developers, as you might expect, were reluctant to build on the land knowing its cemetery history. The city finally stepped in and developed the land to become Forrest Park. Although the land was now a beautiful city park, the citizens were now reluctant to use the park, knowing its macabre history. But eventually some people began using the park to have Sunday afternoon picnics on the old cemetery grounds. Finally, in 1917, the school board acquired the land and built the Beaux Arts–style school building that is still the high school today. The building retains many of its impressive original mosaics and architectural features.

But what about those graves that were believed to have been left behind? Although no stories of ever finding skeletal remains have been reported on the property, it's not unthinkable that remains could have been found when the school was built, and any remains discovered would have been quietly moved or even disposed of. Perhaps remains still exist on the grounds and have yet to be found.

One might think that the school would have been haunted ever since its construction, but it wasn't until the elevator shaft was dug out in 1983 that things start to get a little strange in the halls of Springfield High School. Workers were using a small backhoe to dig out the shaft, and workers found what they thought was a large rock in the bucket of the last scoop of dirt that came up. After cleaning away the dirt, they discovered that they had actually found a tombstone. With the stone weathered by time, the only words readable were "Our Daughter" across the top of the stone and "Cut Down but Not Destroyed" carved into one side, suggesting a young girl who died young, perhaps from an illness or accident.

With the tombstone now uncovered, the hauntings began. The ghostly little girl has appeared to numerous witnesses over the years in various parts of the school, oftentimes in the basement mechanical rooms and utility tunnels under the school. But all kinds of ghostly activity have been reported by witnesses all over the high school. Skeptics often claim that the haunted stories are the result of overactive imaginations and students seeking attention and that the stories have just perpetuated over the years. One might expect students to come up with their own imaginative stories of sinister encounters, but there are plenty of teachers, custodians and maintenance workers who all speak of ghostly and bizarre encounters. These people tend to be in the school building later into the evening and sometimes work alone or with few other people around, providing a more conducive environment for a paranormal encounter than a busy setting during the daytime hours. Nevertheless, as a result of the nerve-racking but harmless encounters with the ghostly girl, she has been affectionately named "Rachel" by students at the school, but her real name will likely never be known.

One day, there were a few plumbers working on a water leak in the basement of the school during school hours. One of the plumbers was inside a utility tunnel, hunched over working on a pipe, when he turned around and saw a little girl in a flowery dress with eyelets all down the front. She appeared to be about ten years old. She was standing in the tunnel just a few feet behind him. Startled by her sudden appearance and confused as to why this girl was down in the basement inside the tunnel, he nervously scolded her and told her that she needed to go back upstairs. The girl turned around and walked out of the tunnel. After hesitating, the plumber, still curious, followed her. He came out of the tunnel just a moment after she must have, where his partner was working. When he turned the corner, he saw his partner, but the girl was nowhere in sight. He asked his partner, "Where did the girl go?" His partner's reply was, "What girl?"

On another occasion, an electrician also working down in the utility tunnels saw the ghostly apparition of the girl, who disappeared right before his eyes. Startled, he came charging out of the tunnel, making a brisk exit upstairs to a hallway full of students, where he pushed by students with a determination to get to the nearest exit. Students said that his face was as

The historical plaque in front of Springfield High School marks this site as the old Hutchison Cemetery. It mentions the high number of child burials in the old cemetery and that likely not all graves were moved. *Garret Moffett.*

white as a ghost. Apparently, the electrician left his tools behind and refused to come back and finish the work.

Rachel's ghostly specter has been seen in the distance, wandering the halls in the evening when there's few people around. Her phantom footsteps have been heard echoing the empty halls. And when anyone calls out "Who's there?" the footsteps suddenly stop. One teacher working late on a club project was walking back to her classroom from the restroom when she saw Rachel walk past her field of view at the far end of a hallway. Every footstep would have echoed in the empty hallway, but no sounds were heard; the apparition just seemed to drift by her view. The teacher had heard the stories of Rachel and gave them little thought over the years but was now bewildered. Rachel was real, and the stories were true for her.

The strangeness doesn't stop here. The home economics room seems to be an area of unexplained activity. Students and teachers both speak of sudden cold spots, sensations of being watched and unexplainable brief gusts of air. One student nervously said that it just felt like someone else was present. There were other people around, but it "felt like someone you couldn't see was there too." In the middle of a test, when the room is normally quiet, a teacher heard the audible sound of a heavy breath or a heavy sigh from someone. She looked up thinking that a student was venting frustration to themselves, but all eyes were down on the exams. She brushed it off until she heard it a second time, and this time she happened to be looking up across the room. No one else acknowledged the sound, but she was certain she heard it. She described the sound as like Darth Vader exhaling. It occurred to her that maybe she was hearing wind blowing down the hallway or through the room from some vent making an ominous sound. Whispers of wind down the haunted halls of the high school wouldn't surprise most anyone familiar with the haunted stories. However, what this teacher had most likely heard was a phenomenon known as the "death rattle," the heavy guttural sound made by a dying person's final exhale of air. Any hospital or nursing home worker would be very familiar with this sound coming from a patient in their final moment of life. This guttural breath is also commonplace in places of haunted activity, especially an area known to be a former cemetery!

Another room known for paranormal activity is the second-floor book room. Teachers work in this room sorting and requisitioning textbooks for their classes. Shadowy figures, cold spots, inexplicable breezes and the phantom sounds of doors opening and closing unnerve some teachers enough that they sometime quickly vacate the room. One teacher who simultaneously saw a shadowy figure standing among the bookshelves and also heard the "death rattle" sound went into a full panic and left the room. She stated, "Whatever it was it didn't want me in there. I don't go there alone anymore." Yet another teacher actually fled the room after hearing the door slam closed and seeing the lights turn off. And although some find the ghostly encounters unnerving and frightful, others find them amusing, even playful. A former teacher mentioned a time when he had set a stack of books down on a table. He turned around to pick up another stack of books, and when he turned back around, he saw that the first stack of books was now split into two stacks, much to his bewilderment. Other teachers speak of similar experiences of books being moved about or books going missing for several moments only to reappear where they were left. It's no surprise that some teachers will only work in the book room with others present.

For some reason, elevators seem to be a focal point for paranormal activity. Perhaps it's the electricity, or it might seem like a fun toy to someone from a time before electric elevators. So, what about the elevator shaft where Rachel's tombstone was found? The elevator here does seem to malfunction at times, but it always passes inspections. When people approach the elevator to press the call button, it's not uncommon for the elevator doors to open on their own, revealing an empty car. Even custodians have become so used to the elevator doors opening that they just say, "Thanks, Rachel." A former custodian said that he was so used to Rachel's pranks and her presence on the elevator that he was not bothered by her. He even joked that he would ask her "how her day is going" when on the elevator. As you might expect, the elevator likes to take people to any floor, but the wrong floor frustrates teachers and students trying to get to class on time. Elevator inspectors are always unable to explain this phenomenon and could only offer up that sometimes elevators just seem to have a mind of their own.

For others, the elevator's strangeness is unnerving at times, especially when a single person on the elevator claims to sense that someone unseen is occupying the car with them. One electrician apparently had one too many encounters with Rachel, so he put his toolbox in the elevator and sent it to the floor he was working on, where someone met the elevator and removed his toolbox while he took the stairs.

For as many times as the elevator doors open and no one is seen, there are also a few cases where Rachel's apparition has been seen walking off the elevator and turning a corner out of sight. For those brave enough to follow her around the corner, they are astonished to either see an empty hallway or people in the hall but no Rachel.

But is it Rachel? No doubt Rachel's grave was not the only grave left behind. It would stand to reason that not all ghostly activity in the halls of Springfield High School results from only her restless spirit. Remember, at least one hundred graves were left behind, forgotten. As a result, one might expect there to be more frightening or even malevolent spirits at the school, but fortunately it is Rachel, the young girl cut down before her time, that remains the dominant spirit haunting the hallways of the old high school. For the students and teachers of Springfield High School, Rachel's ghostly lore has become an affectionate part of the fabric woven into the school's history. Others may have been forgotten, but not Rachel.

There is an addendum to this story. The Hutchinson Cemetery was not the only one in town at the time that was dug up in 1876. There was a large Catholic cemetery at the corner of Madison and Rutledge Streets. The city had a very small and inadequate cemetery just a few blocks to the east of the Hutchinson Cemetery on what is now Adams Street. And there were others. Again, it stands to reason that not all graves would have been disinterred, even though the city ordinance demanded the action.

There is at least one account that comes from the old city cemetery site. The site is now occupied by a modern building and a sunken parking lot area. Employees call it "the Pit." An employee had left work and gone out to his SUV, as he had done five days a week for a few years without anything unusual happening. But on this occasion, when he put his vehicle in reverse, about to back out, he checked his rear-view mirror and was immediately startled by a dark figure that appeared to be standing right behind his vehicle. He turned his head around to get a direct look and saw no one standing there.

Perhaps there are other Rachels out there, wandering the streets of Springfield or haunting homes and buildings where graves were once occupied or remain occupied and lost today.

# THE GHOST OF RUDY

Prohibition was over in 1933, and since then, Americans have been turned on to legal nightclubbing. No longer did people go through the back door to sneak into a speakeasy. The 1940s ushered in a new era of clubbing made popular and trendy by the lifestyles of Hollywood movie stars and famous musicians. The hottest well-known nightclub between Chicago and St. Louis at the time was the Lake Club in Springfield, once located on Fox Bridge Road. Owners Hugo Giovagnoli and Harold Henderson, both of whom had star quality themselves, operated the club from 1940 through 1968. The Lake Club served fine food and stiff drinks, and it had top-billing entertainers to attract customers as well. People also came to the club for the thrill of illegal gambling. Behind a steel door was a secret gambling den where gamblers could play all kinds of standard games. The owners used the gambling profits to pay for the big-name performers of the day.

A litany of stars came to Springfield just for the party and to perform at the Lake Club: Ella Fitzgerald, Mel Tormé, Frank Sinatra Jr., Paul Lynde, Joey Bishop, Nat King Cole, Dick and Jerry Van Dyke, Guy Lombardo, Lawrence Welk, Pearl Bailey, Bob Hope, Chico Marx and the list goes on. Friends of famous performers have also been known to stop in for the party. Mickey Rooney once showed up for dinner and stole the show. Needless to say, the crowd was always at capacity at the Lake Club. It was the place to be, and times were good.

However, behind the glitz and glamour, there were problems for the owners of the club. They sometimes took chances on the entertainment. Once they paid a group called the Vagabonds $15,000 to play at the club for a week, but they only recouped $2,000. But the problems also went beyond the risky entertainment decisions.

Although gambling was illegal, it was somewhat tolerated at the time. After the failure of Prohibition, the law was not overly motivated to crack down on illegal backroom gambling dens. Besides, the Lake Club was far from the only place in town with a secret gambling operation at the time. Dozens of illegal backroom gambling dens could be found in any number of taverns throughout the old Levee District along Washington Street. However, in the 1950s, a new era of social responsibility encouraged law enforcement to crack down on illegal activities. And one night, an undercover state trooper lost $128 playing dice in the illegal back room at the club. Several days later, at two o'clock in the morning, state police raided the room and seized all gambling items, such as a pool table turned over and used as a gaming table, playing cards, dice, IOUs and gambling records. The gambling room was so well hidden that patrons in the club area were never aware that a raid had taken place. The state police raid would be the death knell for the Lake Club.

Without the gambling profits, the owners couldn't pay for the high-price entertainment, so they were forced to hire third-billing performers who didn't attract as many customers. Also, with the gambling gone, the thrill was gone too.

Lawsuits followed the loss of the gambling and plagued the owners, contributing to the decline of the club. One lady cut her hand on a broken ashtray and sued for $23,000. A dancer slipped on stage and sued for $60,000. Irving Berlin and some other musicians sued the club for using music without proper copyright licensing. A comedian was killed in a car accident after leaving the club, and his wife sued. Another patron sued after falling down in an over-capacity nightclub. And on top of all of the lawsuits that had to be paid, there were thousands in back taxes to be paid as well. With each passing year, it was getting harder to keep the doors of the Lake Club open.

The 1960s brought in yet another shift in entertainment. The classy, sophisticated nightclub scene with more intimate entertainment was giving way to venues offering crowds of people loud rock-and-roll bands. An aging Henderson and Giovagnoli just couldn't keep up with the fast-paced and competitive nightclub business.

So, after twenty-eight years, they turned off the stage lights and microphones for the final time in 1968. The owners maintained ownership of the club until their deaths in 1977 and 1988, respectively.

Through the 1970s, there were attempts to revive the Lake Club. New owners opened the Sober Duck Disco and Rock Club and promoted good drinks and quality entertainment, just like the old Lake Club. Not long after opening the venue, the drinks were flowing and the bands were jamming on stage, but almost right away strange things began to happen.

One of the owners commented that the strange activity was minor at first and that they didn't pay it all too much attention. But then he'd start hearing and seeing things and tried to rationalize whether it was nothing or was old pipes or just the old building making strange noises. But the thing he just couldn't dismiss was an eerie, cold chill that would take over a room or breeze by. He said it was a chill that ran right down deep, that he could literally feel his hair standing straight up. He said it was the "worst thing," and he knew there was something ghostly going on in the old club.

Another one of the owners recalled his bizarre encounter with a phantom piano player that convinced him of a ghost haunting his club. He had come to the club about noon one day and sat down at the bar. The main lights were off, so it was still a bit dark in there. Out of nowhere, the piano in the back storeroom began playing, catching him off guard. Slightly rattled, he thought that maybe one of the musicians had come in early to rehearse, but it sounded terrible and he thought he would go back there and see who was playing. He walked down the dark hall to the back storeroom, hearing the piano the entire time; the moment he arrived at the doorway of the room, the music stopped. He looked around and didn't see anyone—just the piano. A cold chill ran right up his spine.

The club owners used another back room next to the piano storeroom as their private office space. Almost right away, they both felt uneasy when in the office. That eerie chill would take over the office at times, and they both had a weird feeling that someone unseen was watching them. They acknowledged a heaviness in the air about the room and sometimes felt like they needed to take in a deep breath of air for a moment to catch their breath. The dog of one of the owners would cower and act nervous whenever in the room, as if sensing something. Electronic office equipment would go haywire at times, such as an adding machine that would sometimes suddenly turn on by itself or go crazy printing out numbers.

Owners and employees talk about the frequently heard phantom footsteps in the back hall leading to the back storerooms and office, but no one is ever seen when the strange footsteps are heard. Owners in the office would hear the footsteps in the hall walking right up to the threshold of the office door and then suddenly stop, but no one was seen. One employee once saw a dark figure in the hall against the ambient light and simultaneously heard the well-known footsteps walking right in front of her toward the office. Nervously, hoping it was one of the owners at the end of the hall, she called out to him. The footsteps abruptly stopped, but no one responded to her call. She said she was suddenly overcome with a nauseated feeling and just needed to get out of there. The unnerving tone of low guttural exhaling sounds could be heard in the back hall and rooms.

Once a bartender went into the kitchen to get a cup of coffee. There was a big heavy steel door that takes a little effort to open and close. He got his coffee and left the empty kitchen, but as he passed through the doorway, the heavy steel door closed right behind him. He didn't go back for a second cup.

Everyone working at the club suspected that they had a ghost haunting the Sober Duck Disco, and it didn't take much research to conclude who the resident ghost might be.

A popular bartender named Albert "Rudy" Cranor, who had been living in a small second-floor apartment, stayed on at the club after it closed in 1968 to do routine maintenance and look after the building. He was

The Lake Club in its day. *From the* State Journal Register.

The dining room and main stage where a number of famous entertainers performed for a packed house for thirty years. *From the* State Journal Register.

a large man with a full head of gray hair. Customers knew him as Rudy, and he had worked at the club for quite a long time. He was a popular bartender with customers and the stars, and he sometimes took them into a small private backroom bar for cigars and drinks. August Busch was one of Rudy's favorite and best customers. Rudy had seen it all, and he was part of the history of the old club. Rudy didn't talk much about his personal life, but people suspected that he had some serious health problems. On June 27, 1968, Rudy sat despondently in a back room holding a high-powered rifle. Moments later, at about 8:00 p.m., he shot himself in the chest and died in the hospital at 6:30 a.m. the next morning. He managed to tell doctors that he had contemplated suicide for several weeks because of his declining health. Rudy Cranor was laid to rest at Oak Ridge Cemetery.

The back room where Rudy shot himself is the same room the newest owners used as their office. Once this information was discovered, the owners realized a grim discovery of Rudy's demise still visible in the room. In a corner of the room, there was a chunk of plaster knocked out of the wall as if someone had hit the wall with a hammer. The hole in the wall looked bad, and it annoyed one of the owners. The hole turned out to be the bullet hole from Rudy's rifle from that fateful night.

Rudy was a restless spirit. As he was Catholic, perhaps his spirit couldn't come to terms with suicide. The ghostly phenomena that occurred, according to a number of witnesses, were unnerving, disturbing and scary at

The back bar room where Rudy would take his best customers for drinks and cigars. This is where a spectral Rudy appeared to a bartender and warned her of the impending death of one of the owners. *From the* State Journal Register.

times. The paranormal activity that occurred inside the old Lake Club was profound and witnessed by various people during open and closed hours, and no one liked to be alone anywhere in the building.

An employee was once bringing in some extra chairs into the bar area when he noticed a pile of dirty tablecloths on the floor. He picked them up and set them down on a table. He went back for more chairs, and when he returned, the tablecloths were on the floor again. It then happened a second time. The third time he placed the tablecloths on the table, he stayed in the bar area and patiently watched and waited; not a moment later, he saw the tablecloths fly right off the table onto the floor.

Employees and customers would hear doors open and close on their own. Cold chills and inexplicable breezes would brush past the bar area, leaving anyone who experienced the chilly breeze unnerved and some nauseated. Phantom music would suddenly haunt the air, startling anyone hearing it. At times, the nonmusical, macabre sounds of someone banging on the piano keys could be heard coming from that back storeroom. When that same piano was on the stage and the unseen hands banged the keys just feet away from employees and customers, some customers would get up and leave without finishing their drinks. Rudy would also tamper with sound equipment control and instruments during performances, making it frustrating and difficult for entertainers. A trumpet sitting on the stage once sounded off with a volley of notes. Static, not feedback, once inexplicably came through speakers during a performance, confusing the sound man. Speakers and amplifiers would turn off and on right in the middle of a performance, causing musicians to take a break to try to figure out the unknown glitch.

Musicians and performers had other encounters with Rudy in the dressing rooms, where the sudden cold spots and phantom touches accompanied by that sense of someone watching them would overcome the rooms. Lights flickered and sometimes went out. Hair dryers were known to turn on by themselves. But anytime that death rattle sound was heard, performers would quickly vacate the dressing rooms, refusing to go back. One musician had a very unusual and profound encounter in that back storeroom, where the piano was kept off stage. Just as he entered the room, the piano started to play by itself, but it was the sight of a spectral hand hovering above the piano keys that frightened the performer so much that he refused to go on stage and perform that night. Worried that he had been cursed, the performer refused to ever come back to the haunted club to play.

The paranormal activity was increasing in frequency, and events were becoming more frightful and mysterious, even dangerous at times. A bartender recalled setting a shot glass down on the bar, and before he could pour a drink into the glass, it suddenly flipped off the bar and nearly hit a customer in the face. Other times glasses would just fall off the bar onto the floor, breaking the glass and startling people. Customers would pause and just stare in disbelief when someone's glass would slide down the bar without anyone touching the glass. People began to get concerned for their safety, as it seemed as if Rudy was getting angrier and more aggressive.

One afternoon, the owners were sitting in their office discussing Rudy and all of the strange activity in the club when a water glass suddenly levitated in the air and hovered over one of the owners for a moment before turning over and dumping water right into the owner's lap. The men had a good laugh this time. Later that day, a salesman stopped by the club and was sitting with one of the owners. The two men sat at a table in the back office going over information. Suddenly, a glass lifted right off the table a few feet into the air and paused before zipping across the room and smashing against the wall, sending glass flying. The owners weren't laughing this time. The spooked salesman scooted back in his chair and looked at the owners in total shock and disbelief. He suddenly stood up and fled the room. He never came back to the club again.

One very unnerving experience by one of the bartenders involved a face-to-face encounter with the ghostly apparition of Rudy. She was in the back bar area, where Rudy had taken special customers, when all of a sudden a ghostly head appeared in the air above the bar and spoke to her. The mouth didn't move, but she clearly heard a ghostly voice tell her that one of the owners was going to die. She described the spectral head as being pale, and she could see right through it. What stuck out for her was the hair. It "was snow white." Rudy was known for his snow-white hair. She was so unsettled by the very bizarre and frightful incident and message that she kept it to herself, worried that if she did say anything about it one of the owners would indeed die. But several weeks later, despite her silence, Harold Henderson, one of the original owners who still had ownership of the building, passed away.

One of Rudy's final pranks was a pretty unusual trick. A customer had ordered a rum and coke. The waitress retrieved the drink from the bar and sat it down on the table where the customer was sitting. As she turned to leave, the man quickly told her that it wasn't a rum and coke—it was a glass of chocolate. She looked at the drink, and it was in fact a glass of liquid chocolate. She was completely confused, as she had watched the bartender actually make the drink properly and had taken it immediately to the table. There was no way for chocolate to have gotten into the glass. Furthermore, there was no chocolate anywhere on the premises. But guess who liked chocolate? Yep, Rudy.

Soon after the chocolate incident, one of the owners was at a class reunion and told a former classmate, who was now a local priest, about the ghostly activity at the club. The priest took an interest in the phenomena and agreed to come to the club and check it all out. The priest showed up with two other priests, and the three did a walkthrough of the club. Nothing happened at first, but when the priests were in the back hall and office area, an eerie, icy chill overcame the men, and one of the priests commented that there was one very restless soul in turmoil among them. He sensed that the spirit wanted to communicate with them. All three priests agreed that it was not an evil presence, but a restless soul, nonetheless. The priests felt that an exorcism was not warranted, but offerings of prayers and blessings would be appropriate. The priests walked through the entire club reciting scripture, sprinkling holy water and offering blessings and prayer. Once in the back room where Rudy had shot himself, they asked God for the repose of Rudy Cranor's soul and to receive him into heaven.

The rites seemed to have worked. Things quieted down at the club, and perhaps Rudy had crossed over. The owner said that Rudy had become part of their club family, even though no one was ever willing to work alone in the club, especially late night after hours. After the blessings, some of the staff commented that they kind of missed some of Rudy's antics, saying that it was like having a practical joker around all the time. But in the end, they all hoped that Rudy had found peace with the help of the priests.

It should be noted in this particular case that the paranormal activity began with somewhat common and expected ghostly activity similar to a residual haunting. However, over time, and with the club open and active again, Rudy's restless spirit became increasingly active and aggressive at times, likely seeking attention and help. It's interesting that no witness every reported feeling like they were trespassing in Rudy's space and that he wanted the people gone, despite some of the frightful events that are typical of many aggressive hauntings. Perhaps Rudy's strength in paranormal activity derives from the turmoil that he no doubt felt over his own demise. Could it be that Rudy's behavior and antics were his way of reaching out to the human side of life for help for his lost soul in the spirit realm, seeking peace for what he had done?

The final chapter of the old Lake Club and the Sober Duck Disco would unfold one early August morning in 1992. When firefighters arrived at the scene at about 6:30 a.m., the building was already heavily engulfed in fire. By 8:00 a.m., the building was destroyed. It was arson, and the case remains unsolved today.

# SINISTER JOE

C ommunity theater is an important part of cultural progress and development, and Springfield's Theatre Guild was no exception. The acting troupe originally held performances in the basement of the Brinkerhoff home. The guild was well supported by Springfield and raised $175,000 for the construction of a new theater building. In 1951, the doors opened at its new theater on Lawrence Street. On opening night, November 6, all 482 seats were sold out for the performance of *Born Yesterday*.

Over the years, the community theater was host to a number of well-known performances, such as *The Seven Year Itch*, *Anastasia*, *Oklahoma!* and even *Our American Cousin*, made famous due to Lincoln's assassination at a performance of it. Performances generally received positive reviews, and the guild boasted membership of nearly three thousand.

The theater guild has since moved into a new location at the Hoogland Theater on 6th Street, where the stage is alive with performances. The old theater's curtain came down, the seats were emptied and the doors were locked for a number of years. Only old ghosts remain. Then the theater was finally purchased and reopened as the Legacy Theater under private ownership. The stage has come alive once again!

The theater is believed to be one of the most haunted places in Springfield. Theater-minded people, like sports players, can be quite superstitious. Since 1955, after an incident, some thespians believe that performances at the old community theater were cursed, plagued by problems, glitches and mishaps. There is a dark and sometimes malevolent presence that has a hold on this old theater. It has made its presence known to many unsuspecting visitors to the theater violating its domain or questioning its existence.

Locations where intense emotions have been imprinted on the environment, such as old theaters, are conducive to ghostly activity. Actors and audiences alike express a wide range of emotions during performances. There's laughter and sadness, anger and fear, love and hate, and over time it is believed that this energy somehow stays with the theater long after the curtains close. Plays often tell the story of some tragedy, yet it would be a real-life tragedy that would set the stage for the haunting of sinister Joe Neville in the old theater.

The haunted history unfolded on the night of May 13, 1955, when an actor named Joe Neville left the theater after a rehearsal, went home and committed suicide by hanging. It turned out that the financial company that Joe worked for had done an audit, and Joe had been the focus by the auditor to explain a substantial amount of money that had been unaccounted for. Unable to face the humiliation of the charge, Joe took the easy way out.

Joe was known by his peers to be a bit of an eccentric and temperamental guy, and he always seemed to have a cigarette lit. Joe was not very friendly with most folks. He was a difficult man of arrogant disposition. But the theater soothed Joe's temperament, and he was clearly tamed on the stage. Joe was said to be a decent actor, and so his colleagues tolerated his volatile personality. His peers also tolerated the strong smell of Noxzema that surrounded Joe almost constantly. He had a persistent rash on his legs, and it is believed that he used the cream as a treatment to soothe the irritation.

Joe's past was, however, shrouded in mystery. It was rumored that he had acted and directed plays in England, where he was from, but under a different name. When Joe left England for the United States, he apparently gave away a lot of land to various people, but there was one problem: Joe didn't own any of the land he gave away.

At the time of Joe's death, he was for the first time playing the lead role in an upcoming performance, realizing his ambition. He had longed for years to be the lead on the stage and on the playbill. But Joe was dead, and he was replaced. The show must go on!

Some believe that Joe was upset that the show went on without him. Some believe that Joe and his temperamental disposition remained in the theater to vent his frustrations on future performances at the theater.

At first, strange and bizarre yet harmless things occurred, like lights flickering or turning on or off. Things became inexplicable, as doors would open and close on their own and unintelligible voices and conversations were

The old Springfield Theater Center, now the Legacy Theater, where Joe Neville still guards over his territory. *Garret Moffett.*

heard, yet no one was seen. Props sailed across the stage right in front of rehearsing actors, and other times props moved about and were not in place when actors reached for them. Attempts to explain events by poor stage managing didn't explain all of the strangeness and were met with skepticism.

Over time, the hauntings escalated. During play rehearsals, a dark shadowy figure lurking and stalking among the seats began to distract performers. Others claimed to see the dark figure sitting in one of the seats in a back row, accompanied by a faint orange glow of a lit cigarette, convincing them that Joe was watching them. During actual performances, actors were also distracted by the shadowy figure in the catwalk above the stage when no one was supposed to be up there. Other actors believed that they could feel Joe's presence on the stage, claiming that they don't feel alone, that someone was watching and intimidating them, especially when unseen hands would nudge or push them. Stagehands and actors began to believe that they had seen Joe's apparition standing in the curtain wings of the stage and became even more superstitious—if Joe appeared to them, their performance might be cursed with problems and receive poor reviews.

Actors frequently make costume changes during the shows. On several known occasions, actors stepped off stage to make a very fast costume change, only to find their costume missing. One time, a costume was later found neatly folded on the floor under a stairwell. Another time, several missing costumes were later found strewn over a ladder away from the stage.

The fact that strange things were happening during actual performances served only to unravel the nerves of some of the actors. Some became more concerned about Joe's onstage pranks than trying to remember their lines, creating uncomfortable moments on stage. One of the most well-known onstage pranks occurred during a performance when an actor answered a phone call as part of the show. When he picked up the phone, which obviously was not hooked up to a phone line, to act out the phone call, he heard static coming through the phone like a bad radio station. Speechless, the actor froze in astonishment. The actor next to him quietly muttered his next line to him, but the actor remained frozen, and it took several awkward moments before the actor recovered enough to return to the performance. The show ended without further incident, but the actor became convinced that Joe had targeted him and his performance.

With each bizarre event, the actors talked more about Joe, and the more superstitious they became. Superstition gave way to fear, and Joe seemed to feed off the fear, so hauntings became more pronounced and frightful. Believers of Joe's presence were convinced that the naysayers only angered Joe's restless spirit; the naysayers believed that all the talk of Joe was in their head and that the haunted activity was still somehow explainable.

But then Joe's angry spirit became downright dangerous. He began to attack people. On one occasion, a stage crew was busy building a stage set while discussing the existence of Joe. The men were sitting on the edge of the stage on a smoke break when one of the men voiced his doubts that Joe was real and claimed that there was no such things as ghosts. Suddenly, a nearby circular saw started up on his own and fell to the floor; several sheets of plywood leaning against a worktable fell over, crashing loudly; and a stepladder scooted across the stage several feet, right before the eyes of the stage carpenters. Speechless and astounded, even the naysayers were at a loss to explain what had just happened. The unnerved carpenters quit work for the night and left the theater, but not before turning on the traditional "ghost light" (a single light left on in theaters, so no one trips or falls in the dark, empty theater). Talk of the incident quickly spread through the ranks of actors and stagehands, causing fear and uncertainty if the performance would go on, but it did.

As the years passed, the intensity of the haunted activity gradually diminished. Performances were still occasionally glitched or affected by petty occurrences—perhaps due to poor stage managing, or perhaps Joe was still seeking attention for a performance that he never gave.

Although Joe had seemingly tamped down or even moved on, the distinct and pungent smell of Noxzema still occasionally wafting through the air would alert and unnerve actors to his continued presence. The use of the cream in the theater was banned years ago, ever since Joe's death.

But the story doesn't exactly end here. In the 1990s, the theater guild moved over to the Hoogland Theater. The shows go on there to this day, and the Legacy operates today under private ownership. But the stories of sinister Joe Neville still linger in the minds of some of the veteran actors. Old superstitions die hard, and some believe that Joe has followed the group to the new location. During rehearsals, some actors are unnerved by the presence of a dark, shadowy figure sitting in a seat in the back row of the main auditorium. If the faint orange glow of what seems to be a lit cigarette isn't convincing enough that Joe has indeed followed the troupe, the unmistakable smell of Noxzema in the air makes believers out of nonbelievers time and time again.

# SPRINGFIELD'S HAUNTED CASTLE

George Brinkerhoff was born in Gettysburg, Pennsylvania, and came to Springfield after graduating from Gettysburg College well before the famous Civil War battle. He became a member of the Illinois bar, and he used his law education to further his various business ventures in insurance and farm loans. He had a short friendship with Abraham Lincoln, but he had left an impression on Mary Lincoln, who asked Mr. Brinkerhoff to be an honorary pallbearer at Lincoln's Springfield funeral.

Using his wealth, Brinkerhoff had a beautiful Victorian Italianate mansion built in 1869, which became known as "the Castle." George and his wife, Isabella, along with their six children, lived in the home; they also lost an infant child in the home. The home cost about $25,000 to build at the time, and it not only served as a residence and a place of entertainment, but the home is also a testament to the success of George Brinkerhoff. The property was originally several acres in size, and George's favorite pastime was horticulture. He constructed a large greenhouse to the southeast of the home. His greenhouse supplied local florists for years. There was also a small dairy once located on the property.

For almost thirty years, the Brinkerhoff home thrived and prospered. The home was host to a great number of dinner parties and social events that were well attended. Upon the death of Isabella in 1894, George held fewer social events at the castle, but he still managed to run his greenhouse and other businesses until his death in 1928.

Mr. Brinkerhoff left his home to the Ursuline Convent upon his death. Since 1929, the old Brinkerhoff home has had many uses, such as classrooms and dorm rooms for a junior college. The basement was once used by the Springfield Theatre Guild as its first theater home. Today, the home is restored, and the social events have returned. The home can be rented out for receptions and activities. Ghosts are included in the rental price. It seems that George Brinkerhoff and others may still be in the castle, not only looking after the home but also playing pranks and socializing with the contemporary guests.

A number of ghostly encounters have been quietly talked about for years. It seems that the most active spirit in the house is quite the prankster and likes to engage in attention-getting pranks on various unsuspecting people. Strange things occur here all over the home and at any hour of day or night.

George Brinkerhoff died in his upstairs bedroom, and most believe that it's his restless spirit that haunts and plays pranks in the house. His ghostly and benevolent specter has been seen throughout the house on a few occasions. An instructor once opened George's old bedroom door, now an office, only to be startled by the faint, blurry figure of a man in nineteenth-century clothing who disappeared from sight right in front of her eyes. It happened so fast that he was gone the moment she saw him; she wasn't sure if it was anything more than her overactive imagination. Yet other workers and guests have reported seeing the figure of a man passing by a distant doorway or crossing a hall, with encounters lasting only a split second. George is thought to be playing his pranks in the library, where he apparently likes to move around books and sometimes other objects, sometimes right in front of unsuspecting witnesses. A guest in the house once reported sitting and skimming through a book when she was called away for a phone call. When she returned to the empty library moments later, the book she had been reading had been re-shelved, much to her amazement. Amused, she had heard of George's antics and called out "Good one," downplaying the incident. The light from a nearby floor lamp momentarily flickered.

People working in the home over the years have reported hearing the phantom sound of a baby or young child crying. The sounds seem to come from the upstairs, but anyone going upstairs trying to track and locate the sounds of the crying was always unable to discern where the crying is coming from; sometimes it suddenly stops altogether. The crying sounds can be unnerving to some, especially mothers, but most agree that it may be the sounds of the Brinkerhoffs' infant child who died from an illness in the

Springfield's haunted castle, the Brinkerhoff home. *Garret Moffett.*

house. But there's also the known sounds of the pitter-patter of children's feet running through the house, sometimes accompanied by giggling.

Other strange and ghostly things occur in the house, as you might expect, such as lights flickering for no known reason and the sounds of doors opening closing on their own. A staff member once spoke about working at her desk and sensing someone else unseen standing there and watching her. It happened several times, and once she even called out for the spirit to stop watching her. Although the sensation left, it would still occasionally return, and she learned to ignore it over time. Perhaps it's George Brinkerhoff himself.

Staff sometimes talk about electronics and computers powering up or down seemingly by themselves. A secretary spoke about occasionally hearing an old-time typewriter clicking and snapping away, but no one typing is seen. She claims that the phantom typist no longer unnerves her and is now just good company, especially on a rainy day.

Even the receptions and social events are not immune to ghostly events. Deejays, photographers and other entertainers sometimes complain about having difficulty getting certain electronics to work properly, but then suddenly they work fine moments later without any plausible explanation. Photographers will also complain about their camera not being able to focus properly on the subject and cameras suddenly being drained of battery power for no known reason. Replaced batteries have also been known to quickly drain of power without explanation, frustrating photographers trying to capture the moments. Amusingly, even caterers have claimed to have trouble with appetizers on trays moving about or going missing, which throws off food counts (this could be simply be a hungry server blaming the missing food on George).

But not all of the haunted activity occurs inside the Brinkerhoff home. Next to one of the old academic buildings is a small parking lot that was once a small cemetery for the sisters of the convent. Remember the city ordinance of 1876 that required all cemeteries within city limits be moved outside of the city limits? These sisters' graves were all moved to Calvary Cemetery adjacent to the north of Oak Ridge Cemetery. And as you might expect, this parking lot has been the site of several ghostly incidents. Students and teachers alike have had unnerving encounters with dark, shadowy figures and specters seen drifting through the area, perhaps nuns wearing their black habits. Some claim to have seen shadow figures in other areas of campus as well. However, a number of people don't seem to be threatened by the shadow figures, feeling that they are just spirits of the sisters still watching over their old convent where they spent many years of their lives serving God's will. The school and convent was a place where the sisters provided others with an education and taught a strong Christian faith for those willing to receive it.

Perhaps the sisters are now earthbound angels who have remained with the campus and the Brinkerhoff home to watch over matters and guide younger sisters and students in their educational and spiritual development. Or perhaps the sisters remain to admonish George Brinkerhoff for his boyish, attention-getting pranks in the castle that Brinkerhoff built.

# ST. PAUL'S CATHEDRAL

Walking past St. Paul's Cathedral, one can't help but notice the beauty of the old cathedral itself and the Tudor-style Canterbury house next door, where church offices are located. Between the two structures is what appears to be a small courtyard, but it's actually a little cemetery of sorts.

There are no known physical burials here, but there are cremation interments here. Each of the square plaques represents someone's cremains, and you'll see walled interments as well. And on top of the little plaques, you might see little stones, trinkets or even coins left behind by visitors. These gestures are just symbolic that this person is still loved and remembered and that the grave was recently visited. This little courtyard is a quiet place of reflection and offers a sense of peace to visitors.

People don't usually regard churches as places of paranormal activity, and some parishioners might think of paranormal and haunted stories in a negative or disrespectful connotation. But churches are not places of despair or evil; they are sanctuaries for all of the goodness and love that God offers for those who seek him. Churches can represent a sort of heaven on earth for people who have lived their lives in service of the Lord, faithfully attending church services and Bible studies and being an active member of a church community. Inside any church resides the Holy Trinity—the father, the son and the Holy Ghost.

In death, one might think of this caliber of person as going to heaven to spend eternity. If some hauntings can occur out of bond and love for a place, could this also not apply to churches and faithful parishioners? In death, can parishioners return to the very church where they felt at home, spending a life worshiping and serving God? It just might be the case here at St. Paul's Cathedral.

In this courtyard of cremation interments, some people do get a sense of being watched or not feeling alone, but it's not an unnerving feeling for those experiencing this. Instead, people have said that it's more like a feeling of being watched over in an endearing or protective way. Are people sensing the spirits of former parishioners or those interred here, or are they sensing the Holy Ghost?

The positive spiritual energy here in this little cemetery is strong. Orbs and wisps of strange lights occur here and are caught on camera time and time again. Many orb photos show clear and focused orbs of solid light, suggesting that they are not particles in the air reflecting light onto the camera lens or other camera artifact. Some take on light hues of color, perhaps suggesting that a peaceful spirit is present and watching over like people sense. Sprites have also been seen zinging through the air in random directions, even around people who are close enough to see the little dots of lights. Strange wisps of light tend to show up in pictures as well. One night, a tour group was treated to a mist-like white fog that hovered over the ground for several minutes before dissipating into the air, which may have been what ghost hunters refer to as an ectoplasmic burst of strong spiritual energy. This mist faded from sight and then reappeared several times over a ten-minute period before finally fading into the night. While the mist was seen by everyone in the group, strangely the mist didn't show up in several pictures that were taken but rather showed up in other pictures taken at the same time.

Dowsing, or using diving rods, is frequently employed here. Rods are known to spin and cross here, and at times they do seem to respond to direct questions. Two opposing people with dowsing rods may find one pair crosses while the other pair pulls apart and even go back and forth, creating a bizarre light-hearted moment. Standard EMF meters will occasionally beep and light up, but more sensitive meters tend to register off the grid. This is when that feeling of being watched sets in for many.

An amazing photograph was once taken here one night with a tour group. A young lady looked up at the second-floor windows of the Canterbury house and believed that she saw something in the windows. The second floor was vacant at the time, and nothing was up there. While taking the photo, she saw a large orb of light go by her field of view through her camera that

St. Paul's Cathedral, where you can find the Holy Spirit. *Garret Moffett.*

appeared to be on the window. But while looking at the photo later on her computer, she saw something else in the photo and enlarged it. She could clearly see the orb of light in the right window moving downward. But in the middle window, she could also see a face and bald head, with the arms and legs dangling down. Once she identified what looked like a curved left wing, she realized that it was a baby angel. Heaven on earth.

# VINEGAR HILL MALL HAUNTINGS

The Vinegar Hill Mall complex was originally built in 1908 as the Edwards & Chapman Laundry. It was known as the largest laundry facility in Illinois outside of Chicago, boasting just over twenty-six thousand square feet. The facility employed two hundred people, and with such a large work crew, the building had dressing rooms, showers and a dining room in the basement for the employees. The laundry facility was also known for its clean water, which was filtered through sea sand inside two fifteen-thousand-gallon water tanks that made the water soft and crystal clear.

In 1927, Mr. Edwards sold out his interest in the laundry business to his partner, Chapman. In 1952, the laundry facility was leased to F.W. Means Towel & Uniform Company. By the late 1970s, the laundry business was in decline, and by 1981, the old laundry building had been broken up into a number of smaller local businesses. It was renamed Vinegar Hill Mall, which is an eighteenth-century term used to describe a district where the fermentation of crops gave off that distinctive smell, suggesting there might be a still in the area making booze. It's unclear if there was such an operation going on here. Having said that, Springfield was known to have a number of stills operating in town during Prohibition. A laundry facility with very large water tanks already in place would provide the perfect cover.

Since 1981, the building has hosted a variety of businesses that seem to come and go, such as restaurants, bars, a nightclub, a pawn shop and more. Unfortunately, businesses struggled in the mall building due to economic and other factors, and it's never really thrived.

There doesn't seem to be any real dramatic or sensational history associated with the old laundry building, but the building does not seem to be short of bizarre and perhaps ghostly encounters today. The building just has an overall creepy vibe to it, especially down in the old basement area where the water tanks and boiler rooms were once located among a small labyrinth of hallways and rooms.

In fact, ask anyone who has been in the basement, and they'll say they don't like it down there. People who have worked in the building say that they've gone exploring down there and something strange happens every time. An employee who worked in the building claimed, "I've been down there a bunch of times and maybe two to three times me and my friends clearly heard someone run across the stage in the nightclub right above us. The club had been closed for years—there wasn't anyone there. But it was obviously someone running right across that stage; that's exactly what it sounded like." There was even a building inspector in the basement who heard the running across the old stage area above him and was annoyed because no one else was to supposed be in that area of the building. He went upstairs to see who had come into the nightclub area. He found no one else around.

Another bizarre occurrence sees clothes mysteriously appear at the bottom of the basement stairs. On the occasion that an employee had to go downstairs into the basement, no clothes were seen at the bottom, but when they came back to go upstairs, they were startled to see a set of clothes or shoes just sitting on the stairs. They weren't there before. One employee said, "I've seen hoodies, T-shirts and even shoes just sitting there." The clothes are described as modern but secondhand, dirty and worn. She said that whenever she sees the clothes, it looks like they've been sitting there a while. She said it doesn't happen every time she goes down there, but it's happened several times. She also claimed that it couldn't be someone pranking her because she would hear them come down the stairs.

There's been a number of investigations in the building. On one such night, the team had come down the stairs and set up equipment right at the bottom. They left the area to go put out cameras, and when they came back to the stairs, there was a T-shirt hanging over the back of a camera case. It wasn't there before, and it didn't belong to anyone in the group.

Perhaps sounds and events related to the old laundry or old store owners or employees still working their trade are still playing out over and over again to unsuspecting witnesses today. Employees of a long-standing business at Vinegar Hill Mall say that they've witnessed more than a few frightful encounters.

A guttural growling sound seems to be a somewhat frequent encounter in various areas of the building, reported by employees and customers. Even paranormal investigators claim that growling sounds show up on EVP recordings taken from different areas of the building. A customer in a business said that she was shopping when she heard a growling right behind her and thought that someone's dog had walked up on her, but after turning around to look, there was no dog or anyone behind her. An employee in the same store said that she's heard the growling several times and that each time she heard it, she got more unnerved by it and began to feel that someone didn't want her there. Soon after that, she began to get goosebumps, accompanied by an uneasy feeling for no known reason. She said that she thought she was feeling the presence of someone that wasn't really there. She even wondered if the growling and the presence were the same entity trying to scare her into leaving the area.

The area where Julia's restaurant was once located seems to be a hot spot for inexplicable events. The restaurant had closed up and moved out, and an employee of another business was cleaning trash up off the floor only to be startled and pelted by someone throwing trash right at him. He was the only person there cleaning up. "Every time I bent over to pick up something off of the floor, something would hit my back, and then the moment I stood up I would get hit in the chest or my face with some piece of trash. I couldn't tell where it was coming from. But it didn't hurt, it was just paper waste left on the floor." He said that after this happened a few times, he just left and didn't want to find or figure anything out. He said, "My gut instinct told me to just leave, so I did. And maybe that whatever it was had wanted me to."

During a paranormal investigation of the old restaurant, two team members sat in a few chairs in the kitchen area to just sit and quietly listen. No one else was in the area. And within a few moments, they began hearing weird sounds. The guy said it just sounded like someone walking and shuffling about the kitchen area, picking up and setting things down. There were scooting and dragging noises, as if some sort of piece of furniture or cart was being moved. Both investigators agreed that it sounded as if someone was just busy doing work straightening, moving or rearranging things in the kitchen. But of course, they saw nothing being moved sitting in the dim light of their flashlights.

Cameras have caught movement. One camera pointed down an empty hallway where very few people ever walk caught something going by, but staff couldn't tell what it was, as the camera went so fast it was just a blur. You could definitely see something go by, and it didn't look like someone running by. But something not shaped like a person flew by that camera. Everyone in the building saw the video, and now no one goes down that hall. No one wants to.

One investigative team in the building, CAPS, passed by a storeroom next to the old restaurant while walking toward the old club area and moments later heard a very loud crash, describing it like a piece of furniture had fallen over and hit the floor. Returning back to the open storeroom where the crash had come from, they found a large wooden desk sitting precariously on top of a small bar table. They expected to find that something had fallen to the floor, but seeing this large desk on top of the bar table was equally perplexing because it was surprising that the table could hold and balance this large desk. They quickly did an EVP session, and the playback revealed a faint angry voice say, "…gonna knock you out."

Paranormal investigators and employees in the building have reported a range of suspected haunted activity, mainly in the area of the old restaurant, the nightclub and the basement. But the common denominator of those interviewed is that they feel the haunted activity results from businesses well into the past and not to any tragic event. However, there may have been one accidental death in the nightclub elevator back in the 1970s.

Edwards & Chapman Laundry, circa 1910. *Sangamon Valley Collection.*

The old Bauer Opera House nightclub is an area of the building singled out by ghost hunting teams, miscellaneous people and even former nightclub employees as very active with bizarre and even frightful events. People conducting business in the building even today take notice of faint dance music heard and are drawn to the old nightclub area of the building to see what the music is all about, only to find that the music goes silent as they walk down the hall to the old club. The club has been closed for years. Other employees have heard the phantom music so frequently that it's old hat to them.

The old nightclub area has an upper and lower level, a dance pit, a glass elevator to take patrons between the levels and even an old crane apparatus that was used to lower eight-foot-wide pizzas down to the tables from a later pizza business. The place was known for the dance parties, live music and even comedy at one time.

A number of stories come from former employees, and much of the noted activity happened late night after hours when only a few people were around. The strange activity seems to be focused on getting attention or even pranking employees.

On occasion, after hours when patrons were gone and waitresses were busy cleaning tables, they would occasionally find a bar glass sitting on a table that had just been cleaned moments earlier. Barstools were put up on tables upside down for floor cleaning. A moment later, one of the barstools was seen sitting back on the floor right side up. One common occurrence was that lights that had been turned off would later be found to be turned on. Lights would occasionally flicker for no known reason. One former employee talked about an argument he had with another employee about who had turned on the music in the DJ booth, with both men denying it. A former employee said that she would come in to open the bar and find that the lights were already on, which was confusing because she was the one who turned them off the night before. She said this happened several times.

Other former employees said that they never really thought of the place as haunted, even though it can be kind of creepy late at night. They attributed the strange events to old pipes and the settling of an old building; the electricity probably wasn't exactly up to code. But others swore that there was something going on here and that whatever it was it was mischievous.

The most sensational story uncovered here has to do with the glass elevator. Elevators in haunted buildings seem to always have similar stories: the elevator doors open and close on their own without anyone pressing buttons, the elevator takes patrons to a different floor than the one requested, uneasy feelings are felt inside, that kind of thing. And the glass elevator here has those stories as well, but this elevator is said to have an apparition that rides the elevator up and down. Witnesses in the old nightclub well after hours and patrons have said that it wasn't too uncommon to see the elevator transport itself without anyone seemingly on board. People said it was a little unnerving at first but that you just kind of get used to seeing the doors open and close by themselves and the elevator moving without anyone. A former employee said that if the elevator was moving, you didn't look at it. You don't want to see her.

But one old bar employee told a story:

> *It was four in the morning there was only 3 to 4 four of us finishing the cleanup and the lights were up, no one was near the glass elevator, and I could see right inside, no one was in there, and suddenly there it goes right up the second-floor landing on its own again. I didn't think too much of it, but this time I was annoyed or uneasy by it and I turned and looked up at the landing, and there was this white gas or maybe a cloud of something drifting out of the open doors and then it was gone as fast as the moment I saw it. I wasn't even sure I saw it, but I sure saw something. I looked around and the other employees were doing their own thing. I didn't say anything, but I wanted to. We all disliked that elevator, none of us liked using it, but I don't know what I saw and didn't want to make myself look stupid. It took me a few days to forget about it. A few months later the same late-night bar cleanup story, this time one of the waitresses chose to take the elevator up to the second level and moments later she full on screams in terror and runs off the elevator screaming and cussing, and she came running down the stairs so fast nearing falling—she was in full panic. We tried calming her down, but she would look at the elevator and just shake her head and say "Nope, nope." She wouldn't talk. Several days later she finally said that someone had grabbed her, but she just thought she bumped the wall, but a second later she felt firm hands press down on both of her shoulders and heard someone whisper something into her ear, and it made her freak out. I never saw any employee take that elevator again after everyone in the bar found out. Neither did I. But one night I'll tell ya I swear I saw what looked like a short skinny woman standing at the railing up there except I couldn't seem to focus in on her, and then whatever I saw was gone just like that. The elevator doors were closed but she was right there. I was drinking that night pretty heavy and maybe my mind was tricking me, I*

*don't know, but I never rode that elevator. And I don't mind saying I felt a sense of peace when I took another job. I never realized how much I disliked that place until I was gone from there.*

The details are sketchy, but in the 1970s, a young woman partying the night away in the club fell to her death, perhaps when she fell over the upper landing railing right next to the elevator. In another version, the elevators doors opened, and she stepped into an empty shaft as the elevator was still on the lower level. A number of people recalled the accident, but no one could remember the details specifically.

# THE GOVERNOR'S MANSION HAUNTING

In 1839, when Springfield became the capital city, the Executive Mansion for Illinois originally stood at the corner of 8th and Capitol Avenue, just one block north of Lincoln's home. But this house was inadequate, only suitable for small family use, without any office space for the governor or staff. In 1840, Abraham Lincoln proposed a bill that would allocate funds to build a new governor's mansion, but the bill didn't pass. It wouldn't be until 1855 that the new Italianate-style mansion was built, and Governor Joel Matteson would be the first governor in residence at the new mansion site on Jackson Street between 4th and 5th.

The entire area surrounding the new Executive Mansion, known as Aristocracy Hill, was once home to dozens of large Italianate- and later Georgian-style mansions, with towers, widow's peaks, gingerbread, balconies and other impressive architectural features. Unfortunately, they were all torn down over the years in the name of progress and modernization.

The mansion is known as the third-oldest occupied governor's mansion in the country. It's also the "people's house," and when the mansion is open, there is public access to three floors. People can walk through four different parlors, four bedrooms that can be rented out, a ballroom and a large formal dining room with crystal chandeliers and an impressive table layout. There's even a Lincoln Bedroom upstairs in the mansion; however, Lincoln never stayed in the room or even stayed in the mansion as president. Perhaps two of the most impressive features of the house are the center spiral staircase that winds its way up and a library with features hand-carved from native American black walnut. The house is adorned with incredible historical pieces, such as a gaming table with thousands of pieces of inlay that was once owned by Lincoln, as well as artwork painted and crafted by Illinois artisans.

Considering the age of the house, think of all of the state or even national history events that this mansion would have been witness to, especially during the Civil War, in which Illinois politics and troops played significant roles. Imagine the conversations, the heated debates, the guest list and all of the back-channel conversations woven into the fabric of the mansion's history. Giants in American history have passed through the mansion doors, such as President Ulysses S. Grant, President Rutherford B. Hayes, President McKinley, President Hoover, President Franklin Roosevelt, General William Sherman, President Lincoln's son Robert, "Buffalo Bill" Cody and Annie Oakley to name a few.

The events of the Civil War are probably the most controversial and emotional moments to have played out in the mansion. During the war, it was home to Governor Richard Yates; his wife, Helen; and daughter, Catherine. It was no doubt a trying time for everyone. Perhaps no more trying than for Mrs. Yates, who apparently worked hard to maintain a high level of decorum and social status within the mansion during the war. In other words, the dinner parties and politics continued despite the war, demonstrating to the enemy that Illinois was still in control and had plenty of resources. She must have had to put on her game face, and it probably wasn't always an easy task.

Haunted activity is often believed to occur in places where intense emotions may have been somehow imprinted on that environment, and the Illinois Governor's Mansion would be no exception.

There are those who believe that Mrs. Yates still sometimes returns to the Governor's Mansion to check in on things, particularly her old bedroom, where her portrait hangs. It's been suggested that she's unhappy with stained and torn wallpaper in the bedroom. Former staff mention that her presence can be quite strong in the room, and you feel watched—not just that someone unseen is standing there, but rather you feel scrutinized, as if someone is right on you. Tourists passing through the room comment that they don't like it in there and usually only stay a moment or two. One staffer said that she would sometimes see a tourist exit the old bedroom and just shiver for a moment, as if they're brushing a chill off them. Staff also note that although this room can be rented out, it's always the last room rented, and it's not uncommon for anyone who stays in the room to request a room

Early photograph of the Illinois Governor's Mansion. *Sangamon Valley Collection.*

change the following night, if possible, usually citing an uncomfortable bed. But staff and room guests have both reported hearing talking in the room, but no one is ever seen.

But the old bedroom upstairs is not the only room singled out where bizarre events take place. The governor's office on the lower level is also known for strange activity. The bizarre events seem to happen in spurts. Months would go by, and nothing would happen, but then there would be a string of strange things. There's no shortage of former staff members who have said that they don't like being in the office area alone. Staff acknowledge that it's an old house, but there's "settling" noise and then there's things that just don't make sense. One witness said, "How do you explain hearing whispers and people talking? You know you can hear it, but no one is seen. That's not a house settling." And sometimes people feel as if someone is watching them. There's the usual and expected pranks with lights flickering or turning off on their own, smoke alarms sounding for no reason and various electronics glitching or failing to work at times, but these things can all have other explanations. Even state troopers monitoring security from the lower-level rooms have heard the whispers and talking and seen the lower-level outside door open as if someone just walked in, but no one is seen.

An Illinois state trooper was once trapped in the mansion elevator for four hours under suspicious circumstances. It was said that the elevator electronics were not working right, and the elevator would sound like it's powering up and jerk but never moved, as if something was preventing it from moving or opening the doors. Once rescued, the trooper was clearly rattled by the experience. It's reported that the trooper said he was not alone in that elevator. On another occasion, a trooper sitting in the office area was suddenly startled by a loud crash in a nearby hallway where the elevator was located. He said it sounded like a metal trash can had been thrown down on the tile floor. When he got to the hallway where the crash came from, there was no metal trash can to be seen, but the elevators doors were standing wide open, waiting for someone to step on board. For whatever reason, Mrs. Yates seems to like to prank the troopers from time to time.

A secretary once allegedly saw a pen pop up right out of the holder and plop on the governor's desk. She turned to immediately walk out of the room, and when she looked back the pen was nowhere to be seen. When she came back into the room later, the pen was seen back inside the holder. She also commented that the room was frequently cold, but she thought nothing of it—just the AC doing its job. She would occasionally hear noises coming from the room but explained them as an old building settling, doing her best to ignore the noise that sounded like someone was in the office. But she also said that she finally realized she was always annoyed and a little irritated when she had to go into the office.

Rumor has it that the governor himself witnessed a book get pushed off his desk onto the floor by unseen hands. Later administrations don't seem to have much to say about any haunted activity. Perhaps the activity just faded away, or is it that no one is talking?

IN 1963, THE ILLINOIS HOUSE of Representatives voted to tear down the old mansion rather than put the money into the needed repairs. The intent was to then build a modern house somewhere in a residential neighborhood. Illinois preservation groups stepped in to save the mansion from demolition. But it wouldn't be until 1976 that the Illinois Executive Mansion was placed in the National Register of Historic Places, helping ensure that the home can no longer be torn down.

In 2016, Illinois governor Bruce Rauner and his wife announced that a $15 million renovation of the mansion and property would take place at no cost to Illinois taxpayers. Today, the Illinois Governor's Mansion stands, casting a stately presence over downtown Springfield.

# GHOSTS OF THE CURVE INN

In 1926, the federal government established the national highway system, and the highway from downtown Chicago to Santa Monica, known as Route 66, was created. Also affectionately known as the Mother Road, the legendary highway would pass right through Springfield, Illinois. The highway became a part of Americana, and with it came myths, legends and ghosts.

There would be a total of three Route 66 road alignments through Springfield for motorists. The original and first Route 66 into Springfield brought motorists into town on north Peoria Road, right past the east gate of the Illinois State Fairgrounds. The flow of traffic brought motorists right into the center of town on various streets through the early Route 66 years, such as 5th, 6th and other streets. The heavy flow of traffic into town created traffic congestion and led to the need to move traffic away from the city center to flow better through town. The second Route 66 road alignment added was 9th Street, moving traffic right by St. John's Hospital, the Lincoln Depot and the Lincoln home site. Tourists began stopping at the depot and the Lincoln home, making the president's house and depot where he gave his famous Farewell Address all part of the Route 66 allure.

By this time, businesses that catered to the needs of motorists such as gas stations, auto shops, family restaurants and road motels were popping up all along the route. And with the growing popularity and ease of road travel, more motorists and tourists poured through Springfield headed westward on the open road across America.

In late 1920s, the final south and third road alignment of Route 66 through town was created, and the 9th Street corridor running through south of town made a large curve in the road where the Curve Inn stands today. The route soon became known as the "City 66." This curve in the road slowed traffic a little, and it seemed like a good spot for businesses. The Copp family soon built a number of buildings and businesses to serve the passing motorists, and the curve was soon established as Copp's Corner. There was a gas station, auto shop, grocery store and even some cabins for travelers. The old Comerford Inn at the curve was purchased by the Copp family in 1932, and they ran the roadhouse where travelers could get off the road for food and drink. In 1945, the building was purchased and renamed the Curve Inn because of the curve in the road that ran past the old roadhouse.

At the time, roadhouses, as they were called, were more than just places of respite and food and drink. Many were also known for illegal vices such as backroom gambling and prostitution. There were scandals and debauchery. The Curve Inn at Copp's Corner was no exception. For example, there was a secret buzzer under the back stairs where customers could gain access to the girls waiting upstairs in the rooms above the bar area. With this type of vice comes disagreements and fights between customers and the working girls. In several cases, the fights led to murder at the Curve Inn. Details are sketchy, but there were several prostitutes murdered here in the early days. And there were fights in the bar area, with one fight leading to a man being stabbed to death at one corner of the bar.

In one case, a working girl was kidnapped by an angry, jealous patron. She was later found murdered alongside a country road. She had been strangled to death. Her case is still unsolved. The angry customer was never captured. Some believe that her spirit remains at the Curve Inn, stuck in a residual haunting that will play out over time until her murder is solved.

The backroom gambling and the working girls upstairs are long gone; however, according to staff and customers alike, events of the past history seem to play out at the Curve Inn today through bizarre, unexplainable and ghostly encounters.

There are regular customers who have said they don't like the back room— they don't know why, they just don't like it. Even though the dart boards, poker machines and restrooms are toward the back, some customers don't play darts or use the poker machines and make quick use of the bathrooms. However, one of the regulars said that the back room just has a bad vibe sometimes and that it feels like someone is watching you. Although there are other people in the room, people will say it's a different kind of "feeling watched." One woman said that the room just makes her angry: "If I hang out by the darts, give me a few minutes and I'll get angry at someone for something!" She jokingly said it's best for everyone that she doesn't hang out back there. She said she would sit back at the bar and have no idea why she got so angry. But then she turned serious and said, "It's just not right back there. Someone got hurt back there."

Bar staff and patrons speak of uneasy feelings of a presence, but some bar staff believe that they've seen the ghostly apparition of the man who was stabbed in the bar area: "I've seen him. I was busy with bar work, and I saw him at the corner of the bar standing there about a foot or two away from the bar, but he was just standing there with this empty expression and his hands were at his side. The whole thing just looked really odd, and then he was just gone." Other staff believe that they've seen him in similar eerie encounters. There's a door with a window in it that opens to the outside beer garden from the bar area, and in one frightful encounter, the same expressionless man was seen outside standing in the window staring into the bar in a fleeting moment. The employee said that she just told herself that she didn't see that under her breath and went about her work.

The sounds of phantom footsteps walking across the floor above have grabbed the attention of bar staff more than once. "We'd be cleaning up after hours, all of the employees are right here, and suddenly we'd hear footsteps above us just like someone was walking across the floor. We'd hear it and all look up at the ceiling. The sounds are unmistakable, and you damn well know that no one is upstairs," said one employee.

"I've heard a girl crying before, and another time I faintly heard an argument between a couple of people. It was coming from upstairs. I don't know if anyone else heard it, but I wasn't going to say anything to them," said another employee.

There was a customer playing the gambling machines one evening. He said he could see a girl out of the corner of his eyes looking at him. He described her as in her twenties wearing a knee-length dress that didn't look like the dress of today. She stood there with no expression on her face, just staring at him. "She began to annoy me, but every time I turned to look at her, because I was going to say something to her, but she just wasn't there each time I looked!"

There are employees who won't go upstairs alone, a spot used mainly for storage today. One employee mentioned that the "being watched" feeling people get in the back bar room downstairs is similarly felt upstairs, but upstairs it's as if it's right on you. It can be an intense feeling that makes

The Curve Inn at Copp's Corner, circa 1930. *Sangamon Valley Collection.*

you walk right back downstairs the moment it hits you. She said, "You know someone is there. There's a presence, you just know it, but there's no one standing there." She said it's particularly unnerving to go upstairs when you've heard the footsteps up there before.

The footsteps upstairs are not the only phantom sounds heard in the bar. One afternoon, an employee was upstairs when she heard the back doorbell ring. She came down the stairs and opened the back door but found no one there. She went back to her work, but upon hearing the doorbell ring again, she went back and opened the door. Again, no one was there. Annoyed and a bit perplexed, she went back to work and heard the doorbell ring a third time. But this time she commented to another employee that she kept hearing the back doorbell ring, yet no one was there when she opens the door. Before she could suggest that maybe someone was pranking the bar, the other employee said, "What are you talking about? That doorbell hasn't been wired for years—it doesn't work." Unnerved, she left the bar for the day.

Bar staff and customers seem to agree that the haunted activity in the Curve Inn is the result of those who were once murdered here and that their restless spirits remain behind, pranking and seeking the attention of anyone who will acknowledge their presence. At least a few of the murders are still unsolved today, and perhaps these spirits remain unable to cross over until the unfinished business of solving these crimes takes place.

In 2002, the Curve Inn was sold, but the new owners kept the original name. It's no longer the old roadhouse it once was, with the debauchery and vices long gone. But Springfield's original roadhouse is still a popular stop on the Route 66 adventure west. The Curve is a favorite hangout for locals today. Stop in to experience some Americana, as well as maybe some ghosts.

# ST. JOHN'S HOSPITAL
# AND SISTER BLUE

S t. Francis is one of the most revered saints in the Catholic faith, and in 1223, it is believed that he arranged the first live nativity scene. In 1224, a Seraphic angel appeared to Francis, during which time he received a stigmata, and in the Christian tradition, he was the first person to bear the wounds of Christ. Francis died in 1226 and was canonized in 1228 by Pope Gregory IX; he is known as the patron saint of the natural environment and animals.

In 1844, the Hospital Sisters of St. Francis of Assisi were founded in Telgte, Germany. The order came to Springfield in 1875 and set up its healing ministry in a house at 7th and Lawrence Streets. The sisters' studies to learn English were often interrupted to care for the sick, and in the early days, they were often paid for their services in grain or chickens. But the healing ministry needed a hospital to expand its work, and sisters requested donations. By 1878, the two-story St. John's Hospital had been constructed at the corner of 8th and Mason Streets.

The Hospital Sisters ministry was a pioneer in the medical field and known for a number of "firsts":

> 1885: the first sister nurse to administer anesthesia
> 1886: opened the first Catholic-based nursing school in the United States
> 1899: published the first nursing textbook, which was adopted by other schools

1910: opened the first school of anesthesia for nurses

1941: opened one of the first units for immature babies

1965: opened one of the first intensive care units

1972: became the first trauma center in Illinois

These sisters were also witness to history. It's believed that in 1882, Sister Frances Dreivogt cared for Mary Todd Lincoln in her dying days at her sister Elizabeth's house, once located at the corner of 2nd and Edwards Streets.

In 1908, more than one hundred wounded men and soldiers were brought to St. John's for treatment from a three-day race riot that was raging through downtown Springfield just a few blocks from the hospital. Hospital rooms were full, and mattresses were laid out in the halls on the floors for the influx of wounded overwhelming the hospital. Sisters noted that despite the ongoing riot, once inside the hospital all prejudices, anger and hatred were put aside so that all could be treated without judgement. This is at the heart of what the sisters are all about, the love and healing of people just as Jesus Christ exemplified in his teachings. They believe healing in wholeness—mind, body and spirit.

In 1978, the Hospital Sisters Health System (HSHS) was created, which is a Catholic healthcare mission that works to continue the healing ministry of Jesus Christ. Today, HSHS currently manages a network of fifteen hospitals in Illinois and Wisconsin, and St. John's Hospital is its flagship hospital. The hospital has 457 beds and is the primary teaching hospital for the Southern Illinois School of Medicine. It is also one of two Level One Emergency Trauma Centers in Springfield, along with Memorial Medical Center. St. John's is also home to the Prairie Heart Institute, one of the highest-ranked heart institutes in the country. HSHS also operates St. John's College of Nursing, the oldest Catholic nursing school in the United States, founded in 1886.

At one time, just over two hundred sisters were working as nurses in the hospital. They had a reputation for exceptional nursing care, but also the sisters were known for their gentle comfort. Patients felt cared for, and families found reassurance. But it had to be more just than exceptional nursing skills, for many patients there had to feel a measure of comfort with presence of the Holy Spirit watching over them by the sisters. By the year 2000, there were only three sisters still working in the hospital as nurses, but the sisters still hold some administrative positions today. Today, the sister nurses are long gone, but their legacy remains, as St. John's is still known today for its exceptional medical care.

However, it seems that there is one sister nurse who remains in the hospital, continuing her healing work through Jesus Christ. Stories about a blue ghost nun tending to unsuspecting patients have circulated around the hospital for years. Patients make claims of a smiling sister dressed in a blue habit wearing round glasses comforting them in times of need. Even staff members have had their own experiences and encounters with the blue sister, giving the ghostly encounters validation. Hospital legend says that she's known to be seen comforting people, especially those not expected to survive; perhaps she's there to help them pass on and cross over into the light of God.

Why might a sister who has passed on still remain in the hospital today tending to people? Perhaps the answer can be found in a statement from the HSHS website:

*St. Francis of Assisi devoted himself to solitude, prayer, and service to the poor. He continues to be the guiding spirit for our ministry endeavors. Our compassionate care for the poor, outcast and oppressed is the Franciscan spirit.*

*We are women who have dedicated our lives to and for the love of Christ Jesus, and to our brothers and sisters in Christ. Public vows made to God, through the church and community, are the manifestation of a life of simplicity and service to the sick and poor.*

Perhaps this sister's devotion to the Franciscan spirit that lived through her in life carries with her in death. Clearly it takes a very special and devoted person to live the life of a nun and do the Lord's work. Could that powerful devotion drive her spirit to remain in the hospital today caring for the sick? Paranormal investigators will often talk about how a spirit or ghost's demeanor is often the same as the person had in life. For example, an arrogant spirit was most likely an arrogant person in life. With this sister's devotion to God and the Franciscan spirit and being dedicated to a life of service to the sick and poor, it might explain why her ghost remains, still carrying out her duties.

Here's a story from a patient:

*I had been hospitalized after having symptoms of a heart attack. After running a number of tests, it was suspected that I actually had a blood clot. The doctor wanted me to have another CT scan to confirm the clot. A staff member put me in a wheelchair and took me to the room for the scan. When we got there the nurse noticed the room had not been cleaned up by the previous use of the room. She parked my wheelchair with the back facing the door and she said she would go get someone to help her clean up the room. She walked out and closed the door behind her. I was tired, miserable, and too weak to move and now sitting there alone in the room facing the CT machine I began to cry. Suddenly my chair moved a bit, and I turned my head around to see a short chubby hospital sister in a blue habit with glasses smiling at me. I noticed her coffee stained teeth. I was a little astonished at first as I didn't expect to see one of the sisters and I didn't hear anyone come into the room, but I was a little out of it. She wheeled me across the room to where I could see the TV. I couldn't help but notice there was this gentle nature about her, and I felt comforted by her presence, I felt better. I turned my head around and said thank you to her, and she just smiled big at me, turned, and quietly walked out of the room hearing the door close behind me. My nurse came back just moments later and noticed that I had moved. She kind of scolded me for moving over by the TV citing she hoped I didn't get up and move. I told her that I didn't and that it was one of the sisters who came in and pushed my chair over to the TV. The nurse immediately grimaced her face and said that's not possible, it's Sunday and there are no sisters in the hospital on Sundays. She didn't believe me at all. But my scan and other tests came back negative. But I was still perplexed by my unusual encounter with the sister in blue. When I told my sister about the experience the nurse in the room exclaimed, "You saw her?" The nurse assured me that there were no sisters on duty on Sundays and also told us stories of the sister in blue tending to patients has circulated around the hospital for years. The nurse said she's heard about a number of stories but never encountered the blue sister herself. The nurse told us to go through the pediatrics lobby when I'm released and look at the pictures of the hospital sisters on the wall there. And sure enough there indeed was a picture of the same sister in blue I had seen in my CT room, I recall her glasses and the rosary hanging from her neck. I learned this nun had died sometime in the 1960s, forty some years ago.*

Here's one from a patient and their friend:

*I had a friend in the hospital with a serious illness and she was worried that she might not survive the night. Making matters worse, no family was able to be there for her and I was unable to get there until the next morning. When I came to the hospital in the morning, I was so happy to find out from nurses that my friend had survived the night and that she would be ok, but she was going to be in the hospital for a few days to recover. When*

St. John's Hospital, where Sister Blue still looks after patients, although nuns have not worked in the hospital for years. *Garret Moffett.*

*I got to my friend's room, she was sitting up eating breakfast and she was a bit cheerful to my amazement because she was so miserable just the night before. She told me that a sister sat with her all night holding her hand and comforting her. My friend had been so upset the night before because no family was able to be there for her, but this sister came into her room late and just sat down and started holding her hand. She said it never occurred to her until just now, but the sister never said a word to her all night, yet she remembered feeling of great and calming comfort overcame her. My friend remembered opening her eyes once in a while and still seeing the sister sitting there with a gentle comforting smile on her face. And when she woke up the sister was gone. While my friend and I were talking about it the nurse came into the room and heard us talking and she asked did the sister had glasses. My friend said yep. The nurse asked was she wearing a blue outfit. Again, yep. Then I asked who was she, so we could thank her, that takes a special someone to sit with my friend all night? The nurse, apparently familiar with the nun stories, chuckled and said that no such person works here and that she had no visitors during the night.*

A member of housekeeping staff recalled, "I saw her at the end of the hallway up there once after the floor had been vacated…in the dim light there was this bluish color coming off of her.…She vanished right before my eyes. I don't go up to the 11th floor anymore."

A doctor related this story:

*I had been paged to the hospital for a patient of mine who was to have a surgery early morning. After dealing with the matter, I decided to stay at the hospital that night rather than do the drive home. So, I crashed in one of the doctor rooms on 11th. I remember dreaming heavy that night, but I couldn't tell you what I dreamed about. But I guess when it was time for me to get up my pager glitched and didn't work, the room phone turned out to be unplugged, and no one from my staff woke me up. What woke me up was a tap on my hand. I opened my eyes and saw one of the hospital sisters smiling at me, and then she just turned and walked away. I thought it was odd I didn't think we had nurse nuns anymore. But then I thought maybe she's filling in for someone, but no matter, I was awake and ready to go to work. Later after surgery, I commented that the hospital sister woke me up and I asked who she was filling in for. Everyone looked at me like I was crazy. My charge nurse looked at me cross and said there's no nuns here. I shrugged it off thinking about my weird dreams that night. Personally, I think stories that I had heard through the grapevine had made its way into my dreams somehow. But then being a doctor, I know what I saw.*

According to a patient:

*I had a heart attack and was recovering in an ICU room overnight. The unit was quiet and not much was going on. After a while a sister in blue came into my room and helped me get a drink of water. She was so kind. I kept looking at her blue clothes because I thought sisters always wore black. But we chatted a short while and she told me to be sure to listen to the nurses and follow their instructions and I'd be home in no time. And she left. I drifted off to sleep until morning. The morning nurse came in and woke me up for my medications and in my sleep stupor I asked who the sister was who came into my room last night. The nurse seemed slightly annoyed, and stopped what she was doing and gave me this look of disbelief and said that she was here all night, but no one came in during the night. I got the impression that she's heard this story before.*

A nurse recalled this story:

*I worked pediatrics for 7 years there and I remember a number of times I just knew I wasn't in a room alone though no one else was seen. I could feel someone was watching me, but it was more like watching over my patient. It was kind of creepy, but I was strangely not afraid because stuff like this typically freaks me out. One of my nurse mates once told me that she had seen a sister in blue one time walking out of the unit doors late one night. But one night in the unit it was a slow night and us nurses were sitting around the nurse station telling stories about what we had heard about the blue sister. We were kind of giggling about it, trying not to scare ourselves really. All of a sudden, we heard this loud bang as if a metal tray had hit the floor, we all jumped practically out of our skins. You could hear our hearts thumping out of our chests! Of course, we all got up and immediately investigated the source of this loud crash, but we could never figure what made such a noise. I don't believe we've ever talked about the blue sister ever again.*

A former security guard recalled one strange evening: "I used to be a security guard there years ago. On one of the upper floors were sleeping rooms for doctors on call. Myself, and other guards have seen the blue sister turning corners up there at night. But of course, when looking around the corner no one is seen. We joked about who was going to be the one to stop her and question the sister! I don't think any of us guards wanted to question one of the nuns let alone the one that seems to disappear!"

Before the remodel, there used to be a room 666. The room was an equipment and storage room and not used for patients. One tech said that he'd worked the sixth floor for years and remembered that before the remodel, you could walk by that room and hear equipment being moved around, but you also knew that no one was in the room. He said that no one liked that room, and that staff would find excuses to not go into the room. They began trying to store equipment in other rooms so they wouldn't have to go into room 666. He also said that it began to be a bit of a superstitious thing—walk by the room and make sure that you don't look at the room number or you might have a bad shift.

Is room 666 actually haunted? Who's to say if staff really experienced strange and bizarre activity around this room. The well-known meaning of the triple sixes would produce in most people a psychological or physiological response based on their preconceived notions about the number. Regardless, staff clearly did not like that room. St. John's has been gradually remodeling the floors and updating the hospital, and there is no longer any room 666. The number is skipped right over from 664 to 668. Considering that St. John's is a Catholic-based hospital, having a room 666 probably isn't a good fit for the hospital. Ask yourself if you would want to work in that room or be a patient staying in that room? The hospital sister in blue probably didn't care for that room either.

Although most of the hospital staff have never encountered the legendary sister in blue, some have. Even naysayers acknowledge that the ghostly sister doing her good deeds seems to be an accepted piece of hospital legend and history. Some even speak of her affectionately, citing that the stories of the ghostly sister still performing her healthcare duties are endearing and heartwarming, especially those who have felt and encountered her heavenly presence in their time of need.

Who is this sister in blue? After searching the numerous photographs of hospital sisters, there are a few possibilities, but there really is no way to know for sure so her identity will remain elusive. Her spirit is at the heart of what the hospital sisters are all about—the love and healing of people, just as Jesus Christ teaches us.

# BIBLIOGRAPHY

Angle, Paul. *Here I Have Lived*. Springfield, IL: Abraham Lincoln Association, 1935.

Commager, Henry Steele. *Herndon's Life of Lincoln*. Boston: Da Capo Press, 1985.

Craughwell, Thomas. *Stealing Lincoln's Body*. Cambridge, MA: Harvard University Press, 2007.

Emerson, Jason. *The Madness of Mary Lincoln*. Carbondale: Southern Illinois University Press, 2007.

Fraker, Guy. *Lincoln's Ladder to the Presidency, The Eighth Judicial Circuit*. Carbondale: Southern Illinois University Press, 2012.

Guelzo, Allen C. *Abraham Lincoln: Redeemer President*. Grand Rapids, MI: W.B. Eerdmans, 1999.

Hamilton, Michelle. *I Would Be Drowned in Tears*. Le Mesa, CA: Vanderblumen, 2011.

Hart, Richard. *The Funeral of Abraham Lincoln*. Springfield, IL: Abraham Lincoln Association, 2015.

Holst, Erika. *Edwards Place: A Springfield Treasure*. Girard, IL: R&R Bindery, 2015.

————. *Weird Springfield*. Charleston, SC: The History Press, 2010.

King, Bess. *The Tomb of Abraham Lincoln*. Springfield, IL: Lincoln Souvenir & Gift Shop, 1941.

Kunhardt, Dorothy, and Philip B. Kunhardt. *Twenty Days: A Narrative in Text and Pictures of the Assassination of Abraham Lincoln and the Twenty Days and Nights that Followed*. Secaucus, NJ: Castle Books, 1965.

Lamon, Ward Hill. *Recollections of Lincoln*. Lincoln: University of Nebraska Press, 1895. Reprint, 1911.

Martin, Joel, and William J. Birnes. *The Haunting of the Presidents: A Paranormal History of the U.S. Presidency*. Old Saybrook, CT: Konecky & Konecky, 2003.

Martinez, Susan B. *The Psychic Life of Abraham Lincoln*. Franklin, NJ: Career Press, 2007.

Maynard, Nettie. *Was Abraham Lincoln a Spiritualist?* Philadelphia, PA: Rufus C. Hartranft, 1891.

McAndrew, Tara. *Stories of Springfield*. Charleston, SC: The History Press, 2010.

O'Reilly, Bill. *Killing Lincoln*. New York: Holt & Company, 2011.

Pokorski, Doug. *Springfield Stories*. Springfield, IL: Copley Press, 2000.

Posadas, Rachel Brooks. *Ghosts of Springfield and Southern Illinois*. Atglen, PA: Schiffer Publishing, 2009.

Scott, Beth, and Michael Norman. *Haunted Heartland*. New York: Warner Books, 1985.

Shenk, Joshua. *Lincoln's Melancholy*. Boston: Houghton Mifflin Company, 2005.

Stansfield, Charles A. *Haunted Presidents: Ghosts in the Lives of the Chief Executives*. Mechanicsburg, PA: Stackpole Books, 2010.

Trostel, Scott D. *The Lincoln Funeral Train: The Final Journey and National Funeral for Abraham Lincoln*. Fletcher, OH: Cam-Tech Publishing, 2002.

Warrick, Bill. *The Lincoln Funeral Train*. Tampa, FL: Herron Rail Video, 2000.

## Additional Sources

Abraham Lincoln Presidential Library.
Abraham Lincoln Research Site, Norton.
Capitol Area Paranormal Society (CAPS).
Illinois Department of Natural Resources, historical site brochures/websites.
Illinois State Library.
*Illinois Times*.
Personal interviews.
SangamonLink.
Sangamon Valley Collection.
*State Journal-Register*.

# About the Author

Garret Moffett is the author of *Haunted Macomb* with The History Press and has been the owner and operator of Springfield Walks since 2006.

# FREE eBOOK OFFER

Scan the QR code below, enter your e-mail address and get our original Haunted America compilation eBook delivered straight to your inbox for free.

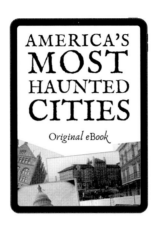

## ABOUT THE BOOK

Every city, town, parish, community and school has their own paranormal history. Whether they are spirits caught in the Bardo, ancestors checking on their descendants, restless souls sending a message or simply spectral troublemakers, ghosts have been part of the human tradition from the beginning of time.

In this book, we feature a collection of stories from five of America's most haunted cities: Baltimore, Chicago, Galveston, New Orleans and Washington, D.C.

### SCAN TO GET
### *AMERICA'S MOST HAUNTED CITIES*

Having trouble scanning? Go to:
biz.arcadiapublishing.com/americas-most-haunted-cities